# FIVE ARCHITECTS

# FIVE ARCHITECTS

**EISENMAN
GRAVES
GWATHMEY
HEJDUK
MEIER**

NEW YORK
OXFORD UNIVERSITY PRESS
1975

Library of Congress Catalogue Card Number: 74-16658
ISBN  0-19-519794-1, cloth; 0-19-519795-x, paper

First published in 1972 by Wittenborn & Company

Third printing, 1977

Printed in the United States of America

# Contents

# Preface

Arthur Drexler

This book is to some extent the outcome of a meeting of the CASE group (Conference of Architects for the Study of the Environment) held at the Museum of Modern Art in 1969. The meeting, at the invitation of the Museum's Department of Architecture and Design, was the occasion for exhibiting and criticizing in camera the work of five architects who may, with only a little exaggeration, be said to constitute a New York school.

This book presents some of the work discussed in the 1969 Conference as well as work of more recent date, and it also attempts to establish the ideological context in which it takes place. Besides complete drawings and photographic documentation, it includes a comparative critique made at the 1969 meeting by Kenneth Frampton, an introduction by Colin Rowe which suggests a still broader context for the work as a whole; and two short texts in which individual positions are outlined in detail.

The buildings shown have rather more diversity than one might expect from a school. But in common they have certain properties of form; scale (all are houses); and treatment of material (all are of wood with concealed steel framing). Historically they are continuing what Gropius and Breuer (and before them Richard Neutra) began with their first houses in the United States: the development through small scale residential work of a teachable vocabulary of forms, but this time without some of the doctrinaire restrictions of the German preoccupation with "functionalism."

The formal properties derive first and foremost from Le Corbusier of the twenties and thirties—before the master assumed the role of latter-day Michelangelo—and Giuseppe Terragni, whose handful of marvelous buildings exploited the ambiguity of wall and column relationships his contemporaries tried to get rid of; and Louis Kahn, whose free wheeling use of the diagonal in plan has renewed a good idea too soon consigned to oblivion by the excesses of Frank Lloyd Wright, who invented it.

Brutalism—architecture in blue jeans and other effete mannerisms of proletarian snobbery—impresses these architects no more than Mies' elegant but arbitrarily pure structure. Instead they have picked up where the thirties left off, pursuing what was implied before an architecture of rational poetry was interrupted by World War II and its subsequent mood of disenchantment, restlessness, and resentment. The resentment, we all know, has good reason. We are all concerned, one way or another, with social reform. But the concern for reform has flavored all discussion and criticism of anything that claims to be architecture first and social reform second. That architecture is the least likely instrument with which to accomplish the revolution has not yet been noticed by the younger Europeans, and in America is a fact like a convenient stone wall against which architectural journalism can bang heads.

An alternative to political romance is to be an architect, for those who actually have the necessary talent for architecture. The young men represented here have that talent (along with a social conscience and a considerable awareness of what is going on in the world around them) and their work makes a modest claim: it is only architecture, not the salvation of man and the redemption of the earth. For those who like architecture that is no mean thing.

Arthur Drexler
Director, Department of Architecture and Design , The Museum of Modern Art

# Introduction

## Colin Rowe

"What you should try to accomplish is built meaning. So get close to the meaning and build." Aldo Van Eyck, Team Ten Primer, p. 7

When, in the late Nineteen-Forties, modern architecture became established and institutionalized, necessarily, it lost something of its original meaning. Meaning, of course, it had never been supposed to possess. Theory and official exegesis had insisted that the modern building was absolutely without iconographic content, that it was no more than the illustration of a program, a direct expression of social purpose. Modern architecture, it was pronounced, was simply a rational approach to building; it was a logical derivative from functional and technological facts; and — at the last analysis — it should be regarded in these terms, as no more than the inevitable result of twentieth century circumstances.

There was very little recognition of meaning in all this. Indeed the need for symbolic content seemed finally to have been superseded; and it was thus that there emerged the spectacle of an architecture which claimed to be scientific but which — as we all know — was in reality profoundly sentimental. For very far from being as deeply involved as he supposed with the precise resolution of exacting facts, the architect was (as he always is) far more intimately concerned with the physical embodiment of even more exacting fantasies.

Fantasies about ineluctable change were combined in his mind with further fantasies about imminent and apocalyptic catastrophe and with still others about instant millenium. Crisis threatened; but hope abounded. A change of heart was therefore required — for, if a new world might still rise, like a phoenix, from out of the ashes of the old, it was up to all men of good will to help bring this about; and, thus while a holocaust of conventional vanities now ensued, the architect called upon himself simultaneously to assume the virtues of the scientist, the peasant and the child. The objectivity of the first, the naturalness of the second and the naivete of the third indicated the values which the situation required; and the architect, transformed in terms of this image could now assume his proper role — part Moses, part St. George — as the leader and the liberator of mankind.

The idea was grand and, for a time, the messianic program was productive. The architect found himself to be an enthusiast for speed and for sport; for youth, sunbathing, simple life, sociology, Canadian grain elevators, Atlantic liners, Vuitton trunks, filing cabinets and factories. And his buildings became the illustrations of these enthusiasms. But they became also the outward and visible signs of a better world, a testament in the present as to what the future would disclose; and there was always the proviso that his buildings were the agents of this future, that the more modern buildings were erected the more the hoped for condition would ensue.

The hoped for condition did not ensue. For, when modern architecture became proliferated throughout the world, when it became cheaply available, standardized and basic, as the architect had always wished it to be, necessarily there resulted a rapid devaluation of its ideal content. The intensity of its social vision became dissipated. The building became no longer a subversive proposition about a possible Utopian future. It became instead the acceptable decoration of a certainly non-Utopian present. The *ville radieuse* — that city where life would become intelligent, educated and clean, in which social justice would be established and political issues resolved — this city was not to be built. Compromise and accommodation were therefore in order; and hence, with deflation of conviction, there followed divergence of interest.

The scene was now ripe for the cheap politician and the commercial operator. The revolution had both succeeded and failed. The cautious and the careful could, therefore, now emerge; but, while they could acclaim revolutionary success and repudiate suggestion of failure, there still remained the predicament of 'the true believer' who, above all else, was obliged to detach himself from success.

The camp of success — always eclectic, facile and agreeable — proceeded to modify and to use the revolution. The camp of 'the true believer' — always anxious for authenticity — attempted to work over the results of the revolution so as to make them strange, arcane, difficult; interesting to the few and inaccessible to the many. And both parties were prone, as advantage seemed to dictate, to employ sometimes the polemics of revolution and sometimes its forms.

Thus there ensued that succession of fractional style phases: the cult of townscape and the new empiricism, Miesian neoclassicism, neo-Liberty, the New Brutalism, Team X, the Futurist Revival. Archigram, in terms of which involutions any consideration of architecture in the Nineteen-Seventies must be based; and, indeed, the two camps — of success and 'the true believer' — have, by now, so much interpenetrated, so infected one another, so much exchanged arguments and apologetic, appearances and motifs, that to discriminate either is becoming a major operation.

So much is largely true today of modern architecture in general; but it should go without saying that these remarks do not wholly describe its *modus vivendi* — either past or present — within the United States. Thus, while with regard to Europe, it is possible to argue that modern architecture was conceived as an adjunct of socialism and probably sprang from approximately the same ideological roots as Marxism, in America an indigenous modern architecture was very conspicuously unequipped with any such implicit social program or politically critical pedigree. That is: an indigenous modern architecture was the result of no largely obtrusive collective social concern and its exponents seem scarcely to have been obsessed by any overwhelming vision of either impending cataclysm or of unitary future world. These visions were distinctively European and, in extreme form, perhaps more specifically Germanic; but, whatever their place of origin and concentration, rooted as they were in the circumstances of World War I and the Russian Revolution, they qualified European production as they never could American. In post World War I Europe, the combined promise and threat of *Architecture or Revolution* could seem to many important innovators to be a very real one; but, in the United States, the presumption that only architecture could turn a 'bad' revolution into a 'good' one, that only a Wagnerian recourse to 'total' design could avert social catastrophe, this could never seem to be very highly plausible. For in the United States the revolution was assumed to have already occurred — in 1776, and it was further assumed to have initiated a social order which was not to be superseded by subsequent developments. In other words, with the revolutionary theme divested by circumstances of both its catastrophic and futurist implications, with this theme rendered retrospective, legalistic and even nationalist, an indigenous modern architecture in America deployed connotations quite distinct from its European counterparts. Its tacit assumptions were infinitely less grand. It was clean, efficient, empirically reasonable, simple, evidently to be related to the time-honored Yankee virtues; and while a Frank Lloyd Wright could — and did — claim revolutionary antecedents, could represent his buildings as the natural sequel to something latent and libertarian in American air, as the *Usonian* efflorescence of a politically democratic society; still, in doing so, he proposed no intrinsic challenge to the social order and inferred no scheme of radical social reconstruction. Instead, such an architecture as his was essentially a call for a particular political society to become more completely itself.

But, if the Architecture-Revolution confrontation (whatever value is attached to either of its components) is one of the more obviously unexplored ingredients of modern architecture's folklore, and if any attempt to explore it would, almost certainly, meet with the most strenuous disavowal of its significance and, if it might be possible to demonstrate the action or the inaction of this fantasy, for present purposes it should be enough simply to reiterate that the revolutionary theme was never a very prominent component of American speculation about building. European modern architecture, even when it operated within the cracks and crannies of the capitalist system, existed within an ultimately socialist ambiance: American modern architecture did not. And it was thus, and either by inadvertence or design, that when in the Nineteen-Thirties, European modern architecture came to infiltrate the United States, it was introduced as simply a new approach to building — and not much more. That is: it was introduced, largely purged of its ideological or societal content; and it became available, not as an evident manifestation (or cause) of socialism in some form or other, but rather as a *decor de la vie* for Greenwich, Connecticut or as a suitable veneer for the corporate activities of 'enlightened' capitalism.

Depending on our values, this was either triumph or tragedy; but the presentation of modern architecture primarily in terms of formal or technological construct, its disinfection from political inference, its divorce from possibly doubtful ideas, in other words, its ultimate American qualification, should be recognized as being important — both inside and outside the United States — and as having direct bearing upon developments at the present day. For, by these means, and for better or worse, the message of modern architecture was transformed. It was made safe for capitalism and, with its dissemination thereby assisted, the products of a movement which became crystalized in the stress and the trauma of the central European Nineteen-Twenties became agreeably available to be catalogued — on either side of the Atlantic — among the cultural trophies of the affluent society.

The ironies of a European revolution which, perhaps, tragically failed to make it, do not comprise the most gratifying of spectacles. When these are compounded with the further ironies of trans-Atlantic architectural interchange and their physical results, in America, Europe and elsewere, we find ourselves confronted with an evidence — an adulteration of meaning, principle and form — which is far from easy to neglect. The impeccably good intentions of modern architecture, its genuine ideals of social service, above all the poetry with which, so often, it has invested random twentieth century happening may all conspire to inhibit doubts as to its present condition, to encourage a suppression of the obvious; but, conspire as they may, and however reluctantly we recognize it, the product of modern architecture compared with its performance, the gap between what was anticipated and what has been delivered, still establishes the base line for any responsible contemporary production and, in doing so, introduces the context for consideration of such buildings and projects as are here published.

These, had they been conceived c. 1930 and build in France, Germany, Switzerland or Italy, had then they been illustrated by Alberto Sartoris or even F. R. S. Yorke, would today very likely be approached as ancient monuments; and as exemplary of the heroic periods of modern architecture, they would be visited and recorded. Indeed one can imagine the tourists and almost concoct the historical evaluations. But these buildings were not conceived c. 1930. They are of comparatively recent origin; they are built in, or proposed for, the vicinity of New York City; and therefore, whatever their merits and demerits, such is the present constellation of critical ideas, they can only be regarded as constituting a problem.

For we are here in the presence of what, in terms of the orthodox theory of modern architecture, is heresy. We are in the presence of anachronism, nostalgia, and, probably, frivolity. If modern architecture looked like this c. 1930 then it should not look like this today; and, if the real political issue of the present is not the provision of the rich with cake but of the starving with bread, then not only formally but also programmatically these buildings are irrelevant. Evidently they propound no obvious revolution; and, just as they may be envisaged as dubiously European to some American tastes, so they will seem the painful evidence of American retardation to certain European and, particularly, English judgments.

Now these evaluations will not be made to go away. A grass roots Neo-Populist Americanism will approve of these buildings no more than a Pop-inspired and supercilious European, or English, neo-Marxism; and, given the situation in which opposite but sympathetic extremes will, alike, both smell abomination, it might be best to address arguments to neither of these two states of mind but, instead, to withdraw attention to that body of theory, alleged or otherwise, of which these buildings, like so many of their predecessors of the Nineteen-Twenties and Thirties, may be construed as violation.

With the establishment and institutionalization of modern architecture, not only was much of its original meaning lost; but it also became apparent that it was scarcely that synthesis it had so widely been proclaimed to be. It became apparent that never had it been so much the limpid fusion of content and form, that famous integration of feeling and thinking, which Siegfried Giedion had supposed a symbiosis of highly discrete and ultimately incompatible procedures; and, if the incompatibility between the form of modern architecture and its professed theoretical program, however apparently happy was their brief co-existence some thirty to forty years ago, has now long been evident, it has also been the subject of, in general sardonic comment. The configuration of the modern building was alleged to derive from a scrupulous attention to particular and concrete problems, it was supposed to be induced from the empirical facts of its specific case; and yet modern buildings looked alike whether their specific case was that of a factory or an art museum. Therefore there was no one to one correspondence between practice and theory. Thus it could come to be argued that, from almost the beginning, the buildings erected in the name of modern architecture had comprised an enormous series of misunderstandings; that they had represented no intrinsic renewal; that, ultimately, they had constituted no more than a simultaneously sophisticated and naive re-arrangement of surfaces. Reyner Banham's Theory and Design in the First Machine Age celebrated just this problem and it concluded with what amounted to a repudiation of modern architecture's forms and an endorsement of what the modern movement, theoretically, was supposed to be. And this is a style of critique which, for obvious reasons, has now become very well known. For, at one and the same time, it allows its exponents the pleasures of condemning, or of patronizing, most of modern architecture's classic achievements and, also, of annexing that revolutionary tone which, though it may be ancient, can still posture as new.

But, if it is possible to speak of the theoretical program of modern architecture and to observe how, almost invariably, it was largely honored in the breach, then, by now, the logical contradictions within this alleged theory itself should, equally, be glaring — though, perhaps, it would be more correct to speak of this theory not in terms of its logical contradictions. For in the light of any critical perspective, what we have here is very little more than an incoherent bundle of highly volatile sentiments, not so much the stipulation of a consistent dogma as the registration of a general tendency of thought and the evidence of a highly pronounced climate of feeling.

As already suggested, in its theory, modern architecture was conceived to be no more than a rational and unprejudiced response to twentieth century enlightenment and its products; and, if we subject this theoretical conception to a slight caricature, we might distinguish what is still a prevalent and orthodox position. It may be outlined as follows:

Modern architecture is no more than the result of the age;
The age is creating a style which is not a style because this style is being created by the accumulation of objective reactions to external events;
and hence, this style is authentic, valid, pure and clean, self-renewing and self-perpetuating.

Thus, compressed and rendered absurd, it becomes, of course, difficult to understand how passion could, and can still, revolve around such a statement as this one; that is until we recognize that what we have here is the conflation of two powerful nineteenth century tendencies of thought. For here, in varying degrees of disguise, we are presented with both 'science' and 'history.' We are provided with the Positivist conception of fact (without any great epistemological reservations as to what does constitute a fact) and we are provided with the Hegelian conception of manifest destiny (without any doubts as to the substantial reality of the inexorable zeitgeist) and then, as a corollary, we have the implicit assertion that when these two conceptions are allied, when the architect recognizes only 'facts' and thus, by endorsing 'science,' becomes the instrument of 'history,' then a situation will infallibly ensue in which all problems will vanish away.

But again, although in these notices we may touch upon one of the central motivations of twentieth century architecture, it is only when we introduce subsidiary arguments into this scene that it fully begins to acquire color and momentum. And thus, the idea of relying upon the 'facts,' however ill determined these may be, the idea that when once the relevant data are collected then the controlling hypothesis will automatically divulge itself, becomes very easily allied with the so many attacks upon 'art' (the gratuitous transformation of private concern into public pre-occupation) which, even though 'art' is bought and consumed to its destruction, is typically conceived to be a reprehensible activity. And, correspondingly, attacks upon 'architecture' conducted by the architect have always expressed irritation at the continued existence of the institution and dismay that the item is still to be found available. For architecture, so it is consistently inferred, is only morally acceptable so long as the archiect suppresses his individuality, his temperament, his taste and his cultural traditions; and unless, in this way, he is willing to win through to 'objectivity' and to a 'scientific' state of mind, then all his work can do is to obstruct the inexorable unrolling of change and thereby, presumably, retard the progress of humanity.

However, if we are here presented with what might seem to be an argument for pure passivity, with an argument that the architect should act simply as the midwife of history, then we might also recognize an entirely contrary strand of thought which no less urgently clamors for attention. The idea that any repetition, any copying, any employment of a precedent or a physical model is a failure of creative acuity is one of the central intuitions of the modern movement. This is the deep seated idea that repetition establishes convention and that convention leads to callousness; and thus, almost constitutionally, modern architecture has been opposed to the dictatorship of the merely received. Opposed to the imposition of a priori pattern upon the multifariousness of events, instead It has set re-eminent value upon 'discovery' — which, characteristically, it has been unwilling to recognize as 'invention.' Without an unflagging consciousness of flux and of the human efforts which this implies, without a continuous ability to erect and to dismantle scaffolds of reference, then — so proceeds an argument — It is entirely impossible to enter and to occupy those territories of the mind, where, alone, significant creation moves and flourishes.

The idea can only deserve respect; but, if it is pressed, then like so many ideas which also deserve respect, it can only become something doctrinaire and destructive of its own virtues; and, with its heroic emphasis upon the architect as activist, the notion of architecture as ceaseless moral experiment must now be subjected to the presence of yet another equally coercive but contrary proposition. This, quite simply, is the idea that modern architecture was to instigate order, that it was to establish the predominance of the normative, the typical and the abstract.

However we may estimate the record of nineteenth century building, it is not hard to see how ideas of order and type should have recommended themselves to the modern movement. For, in contrast to the products of Romantic individualism and political laissez faire, there was always the evidence of previous centuries, of Bath or Potsdam, Amsterdam or Nancy; and, there was always involved some sort of fantasy concerned with a contemporary simulacrum of just such cities as these, then, in the siedlungen of Frankfurt or at Siemenstadt, among the early triumphs of modern architecture, one may presumably discern the influence of this intention.

But such developments belonged to the age of innocence; and while in them the reasonable demands of the particular versus the abstract, of specific function versus general type might seem to have been approximately met, there still remained to prevent the multiplication of such achievements the overriding inhibition as to repetition, the conviction that to reproduce something, to allow precedent to enforce itself, was to betray the forces of change and to deny the drive of history.

Now whether it was thus that the demand for order became vitiated by the competing necessity to illustrate the action of experiment or the behavior of 'first' principles, it should be enough to state that it seems likely — whatever value we may wish to attribute to change and order — that a high valuation of change must, in the end, cancel out a high valuation of order, that, given the perpetual re-definition of a situation, no theory of types can survive, that, if the terms of a problem are constantly altered before approaching solution, then that problem never can be solved. But if, with this statement, though it is rarely made, there is nothing remarkable announced, then attention might usefully be directed towards another of those paradoxes which sprout so irresistibly the more the theory of modern architecture is, even casually, scrutinized.

Modern architecture professed to address itself to the great public. What was believed to be its intrinsic rationality was never overtly intended for the delectation of minor professional interest groups; but rather the architect was to address himself to *the natural man*. Enlightenment won by bitter struggle was to speak to enlightenment which was innate. As simply a scientific determination of empirical data modern architecture was to be understood by *the natural man*; and hence that the modern building, believed to be purged of mythical content, became conceivable as the inevitable shelter for a mythical being in whose aboriginal psychology myth could occupy no place.

The notion, of course, continues to possess a certain eighteenth century decency. Without rhetoric, the truth will be accepted as the truth. But, in practice, it has always allied with an alternate ambition. The modern building should — and can — act as a phrophetic statement. Retrospection is to be tabooed; the memory is to be exercised no more; nostalgia can only corrupt; and it is with reference to this ambition, perhaps never explicity uttered, that we revert again to the thesis of an architecture which does not involve itself with minor sophistications, which is no way concerned with local ambiguities, ironical references and witty asides, which is absolutely not at all addressed to the few, but which, of its nature, is absolutely available and intelligible to the uninstructed (or to the however instructed) many. For there should be no doubt whatsoever that this was the objective, and it is here, when the ideal of public intelligibility makes its extreme claim, that it might be proper to obtrude the issue of prophecy versus memory.

The concept of the modern building as a compilation of recognizable empirical facts is, evidently, immediately compromised by the more suppressed concept of the building as a prophetic statement (for are prophetic speculations empirical facts?); but the simultaneous orientation towards both the prophetic and the intelligible should now be related to modern architecture's emphatic anathema of retrospec-

tion and its products. And it should not be necessary to itemize the details of this anathema. Simply it should be enough to ask the question: *How to be intelligible without involving retrospection?*; and, without being unduly sententious, it should be enough to observe that except in terms of retrospection, in terms of memory upon which prophecy itself is based, upon recollection of words with meaning, mathematical symbols with values and physical forms with attendant overtones, it is difficult to see how any ideal of communication can flourish. In a better world, no doubt, the problem would not exist; but if, in conceiving a better world, modern architecture here conceived no problem, then we might abruptly conclude this issue by suggesting that, unless a building in some way or other evokes something remembered, it is not easy to see how it can enlist even a shred of popular interest. The ideal of order based upon public understanding if it is to be insisted upon, requires some suppression of both experimentalist and futurist enthusiasm.

The foregoing remarks have been an attempt, admittedly overcompressed and far too generalized, to identify — not without critical asides — the complex of sentiments about architecture in terms of which the buildings here published are likely to be condemned — for formalism, bourgeois lack of conscience, esoteric privacy and failure to keep pace with the social and technological movement of the age. But the moment that this body of ideas is subjected to even the most casual skeptical analysis, the moment that it ceases to be unexamined gospel, then it also becomes evident that, while it may serve to illustrate what was once a creative state of mind, it can no longer very seriously serve the purposes of useful criticism. The theoretical presumptions of modern architecture, located as they once were in a matrix of eschatological and utopian fantasy, began to mean very little when the technological *and* social revolution whose imminence the modern movement had assumed failed to take place. For with this failure, if it became obvious that theory and practice were disrelated, it could also become apparent that theory itself was never so much a literal directive for the making of buildings as it was an elaborately indirect mechanism for the suppression of feelings of guilt: guilt about the products of the mind — felt to be comparatively insignificant, guilt about high culture — felt to be unreal, guilt about art — the most extreme anxiety to disavow the role of private judgment in any analytical or synthetic enterprise. In the end what is understood as the theory of modern architecture reduces itself to little more than a constellation of escapist myths which are all active in endeavouring to relieve the architect of responsibility for his choices and which all alike combine to persuade him that his decisions are not so much his own as they are, somehow, immanent in scientific, or historical, or social process.

And this realization breeds another. For if these once convincing and still seductive doctrines — with their strong determinist and historicist bias — are very readily susceptible to demolition, and if they are not yet demolished is surely a tribute to modern architecture's public virtues, then one might still ask why it is that an attitude of mind which places so much emphasis upon change, which sets such a high value upon exploration and discovery, itself continues *not* to change. The *sense* of what was said some fifty years ago prohibits repetition; but then the *repetition* of what was said persists. . . .

Now, either statements made about architecture in the Nineteen-Twenties comprise an immutable revelation valid for all time (which is contrary to the meaning of these statements), or they do not. But if, logically — in terms of the principle which it tends to stipulate — the use and re-use of verbal or polemical model deriving from the Nineteen-Twenties should be conceived as subject to the same reservations as the use of a physical model belonging to the same years, then that such logic does not widely apply is easy to explain. For, while the forms of words can still seem to provide an heroic litany of revolution, the form of buildings does not so readily offer itself as any religious intoxicant; and, if the steady incantation of, now, very old 'revolutionary' themes will encourage the further joys of rhetorical excursion into areas of assumed social and technological relevance, the recapitulation of the themes of building offers no present career so blissful and free from trouble; and thus, while the derivative argument continues to thrive, its exponents, conceiving themselves to be the legitimate and sole heirs of the modern movement, display very little tolerance for what ought to be recognized as the absolutely parallel phenomenon of the derivative building.

Which is again to establish that the *physique* and the *morale* of modern architecture, its flesh and its word, were (and could) never be coincident; and it is when we recognize that neither word nor flesh was ever coincident with itself, let alone with each other, that, without undue partiality, we can approach the present day. For under the circumstances what to do? If we believe that modern architecture did establish one of the great hopes of the world — always, in detail, ridiculous, but never, *in toto,* to be rejected — then do we adhere to *physique*-flesh or to *morale-word*?

To repeat: this choice became visible once it became almost too evident to bear that the central and socialist mission of modern architecture had failed — or, alternatively, that this mission had become dissolved in the sentimentalities and bureaucracies of the welfare state. The simple fusion of art and technology, of symbolical gesture and functional requirement was now not to be made; and, in default of this fusion, a variety of alternatives have offered themselves.

These have included what has already been listed: Miesian neoclassicism (with some kind of dependent theory of Platonic form); the New Brutalism (with the inference that self-flagellation may elicit the better world); the Futurist Revival (with the very popular supposition that science fiction might provide the ultimate hope); and the neo-*art nouveau* (which, both in its Shingle Style and Italian ramifications, insists that if we only retreat to the Eighteen-Nineties — and also simulate a naivete — then health will inevitably ensue.

And, to this catalogue, there must also be added the notion that we ignore the situation altogether: that, in default of that convenient anti-'art' entity of the Twenties called 'the machine,' we substitute the equally useful entities designated 'the computer' and 'the people' and that, if these two abstractions are absolutely at variance with each other, we will not indulge ourselves in too many scruples about this problem. It is a problem which exists only in the minds of the far too sensitive; and if research and data-collection are the wave of the future — if the public wisdom so indicates — then it is certainly to the future we belong.

It is in this context of choices (none of them very agreeable) that we should place what is here published; and, having recognized this context, we should not then be too ready to impute charges of irresponsibility. It is difficult to generalize the work of these five architects. Eisenman seems to have received a revelation in Como; Hejduk seems to wish affiliation both to Synthetic Cubist Paris and Constructivist Moscow. Nor will the more obviously Corbusian orientation of Graves, Gwathmey and Meier so readily succumb to all encompassing observations. But, for all this, there is a point of view shared which is quite simply this: that, rather than constantly to endorse the revolutionary myth, it might be more reasonable and more modest to recognize that, in the opening years of this century, great revolutions in thought occurred and that then profound visual discoveries resulted, that these are still unexplained, and that rather than assume intrinsic change to be the prerogative of every generation, it might be more useful to recognize that certain changes are so enormous as to impose a directive which cannot be resolved in any individual life span.

Or, at least, such would seem to be the argument. It concerns the plastic and spatial inventions of Cubism and the proposition that, whatever may be said about these, they possess an eloquence and a flexibility which continues now to be as overwhelming as it was then. It is an argument largely about the physique of building and only indirectly about its morale; but, since it should also be envisaged as some sort of interrogation of the mid-twentieth century architect's capacity to indulge his mostly trivial moral enthusiasm at the expense of any physical product, it might also be appropriate to conclude what has been a largely negative introduction — an attack upon a potential attack — with a series of related questions which might, ambiguously, help to establish the *meaning* — if any — in Aldo Van Eyck's terms, of what is here presented.

- Is it necessary that architecture should be simply a logical derivative from functional and technological facts; and, indeed, can it ever be this?

- Is it necessary that a series of buildings should imply a vision of a new and better world; and, if this is so (or even if it is not) then how frequently can a significant vision of a new and better world be propounded?

- Is the architect simply a victim of circumstances? And should he be? Or may he be allowed to cultivate his own free will? And are not culture and civilization the products of the imposition of will?

- What is the *zeitgeist;* and, if this is a critical fiction, may the architect act contrariwise to its alleged dictates?

- How permissible is it to make use of precedent; and therefore, how legitimate is the argument that the repetition of a form is a destruction of authenticity?

- Can an architecture which professes an objective of continuous experiment ever become congruous with the ideal of an architecture which is to be popular, intelligible, and profound?

These are reasonably important questions which it is ostrich-like not to consider. They propound problems which are not any less real because the 'theory' of modern architecture failed to give them attention; and, by the introduction of such problems, there is immediately implied a concept of society very radically different from that which modern architecture presumed. This is the concept of society and building implied by our five architects. It is all indisputably bourgeois (but what, in the United States, is not?); most of it makes a parade of cosmopolitan erudition (but, given the information explosion, how to avoid?); and it is all of it belligerently second hand, what Whitehead called 'novelty in the use of assigned pattern' (but, assuming a present hiatus so far as creative breakthrough is concerned, how do otherwise?). However, perhaps the great merit of what follows lies in the fact that its authors are not enormously self-deluded as to the immediate possibility of any very violent or sudden architectural or social mutation. They place themselves in the role, the secondary role, of Scamozzi to Palladio. Their posture may be polemical but it is not heroic. Apparently they are neither Marcusian nor Maoist; and, lacking any transcendental sociological or political faith, their objective — at bottom — is to alleviate the present by the interjection of a quasi-Utopian vein of poetry. There could be less worthy objectives, less tolerable options; and, in a truly pluralist society (supposing such a society could ever exist) what is here published would no doubt receive acknowledgement — as one possibility amongst many. It is what *some* people and *some* architects want; and therefore, in terms of a general theory of pluralism one must wonder how, *in principle,* it can be faulted. Faults in detail may perhaps be recognized; but faults *in principle?* For, in terms of a general theory of pluralism, how can any faults in principle be imputed?

Which is to suggest that these five architects (who sometimes seem to regard buildings as an excuse for drawing rather than drawings as an excuse for building) are highly likely to be crudely manhandled by an allegedly pluralist, but, intrinsically, a determinist, technocratic and historicist establishment; and which is further to suggest that the apologetic which has here been made is by way of being a critical umbrella almost too catholic in its functions — an umbrella which is not only intended to protect the graphic contents of this book but which is also to be understood as outspread to protect a good deal else, a good deal else which is by no means necessarily comparable in *maniera.*

Colin Rowe
Professor of Architecture, Cornell University

# Frontality vs. Rotation[1]

## Kenneth Frampton

Despite the significant differences of these works, they have much in common. In the first place they suffer from a certain inflation of scale.[2] They imply much larger structures, and at first glance it is difficult to assess their true size, since they are all shown without any anthropomorphic key. In the second place, they all appear to derive from a common cultural base in as much as almost all of these designers know each other rather well. On occasion in the past, some have even worked together, and thus they share a comparable ethos in their respective positions.[3]

I will start my criticism with John Hejduk's House 10 of 1966. It is impossible to know the program in this case since these hieroglyphic drawings are presented without either legend or furniture. The critic is left to make his own deductions as to where the building is, what it is, and who will occupy it. Since there are even no indications as to orientation, etc., it probably insists, more than any other project here, on a formal appraisal.

This scheme represents a new departure for Hejduk since many of Hejduk's earlier projects were based on transpositions of a diamond within a square, that is, on a "spiral" of rectilinear fugal relationships, stacked above each other vertically.[4] Usually these houses were divided into four floors and involved an intricate play of elements from floor to floor; precipitating changes in structure, fenestration, and space. This present project on the contrary is horizontal in emphasis. Any fugal play here takes place between the disposition of the related forms at either end of an elongated mass. It engenders an illusion of considerable, not to say palatial, size due to its horizontal extension. Furthermore, there is a certain secrecy about the main entrance, reminiscent of the work of Frank Lloyd Wright. The designer insists on a very direct approach to the center of gravity of its long mass, yet this is not the point of entry. A visitor has to turn a sharp left in order to enter into the organic shaped foyer, before proceeding to the two interdependent, part "solid," part "glazed," pavilions at the left of the composition.

The left-hand complex consists of two pavilions which establish the first "end condition," so to speak. At the other end of the composition there is a three-quarters circle which constitutes the third pavilion and second "end condition." The left-hand complex comprises an L-shaped pavilion and a three-quarters square pavilion. Both are assembled around L-shaped "armatures," as is the semi-circular pavilion at the right-hand end. One is thus presented with three "living" pavilions each of which has two structural elements in common, namely, a column and an L-shaped wall, as the compound means for supporting the roof. In addition, each has a fireplace as an additional free-standing spatial element. A fugal counterchange is established; for example, the three-quarters semicircular pavilion has within it a circular chimney structure, while the three-quarters square has within it a three-quarters square chimney structure. However, at this juncture the consistency of the system breaks down, for the "L" form has within it a square chimney structure that is aligned with one side of the "L."

A further inconsistency arises from the "code" implied by the formal distortions that occur at the entrance. Here two organic-shaped foyers are set in relation to the three pavilions. One is simply a distension of the entry; the other contains dressing room and toilet facilities. The significance of these "biological" elements is hardly elucidated by the addition of "lean-to" glazed structure parallel with the spine and attached to one of the forms. If one can reasonably equate "myth" to language, there are secondary "myths" evoked here — apparently housing specific content which is but cryptically expressed. Each one of the glass pavilions incorporates a variation on a related theme. They are each connected by a spine which is glass on one side and solid on the other. Various views out along this spine yield different juxtapositions of the pavilions. In its horizontal display of forms and spaces this house clearly recalls the work of Wright, and as with Wright the basic strategy has been to suggest a very extensive inner space through the device of an attenuated horizontality.

Apart from the gratuitous cultural reference to Wright, another thing that strikes one about this house is the frontality of its total mass in contrast to the rotation of its extremities. This theme of frontalization versus rotation crops up, in one form or another, in most of the works presented here. Advancing from the roadside garage in the Hejduk House one is presented with a series of planes, partly denoted by paths on the ground and partly established by glazed surfaces so that this layering of frontal planes is reinforced as one approaches the house. Once within the spine, however, this initial frontalization collapses like a mirage into the axis of its labyrinthine organization.

A very different situation obtains in Peter Eisenman's House I, the Barenholtz Pavilion in Princeton, where the play between frontalization and rotation amounts to an ever present conflict which at no point is ever allowed to be resolved. Intimations of frontality and assymetrical spinning are present constantly. Neither inside nor out is the one allowed to become master over the other, although paradoxically, in comparison to the Hejduk House, the building is not approached frontally. The museum entry is arranged in such a way that, to the initiated, it is reminiscent of the approach to Terragni's Giuliani-Frigerio, in Como, where there is insufficient depth to permit frontalization.[5] Willfully obscured, the museum is based on an infrastructure which amounts to an overlay of tartan grids running in two directions. These grids generate a number of augmenting and conflicting planes. Apart from the contrasting phenomena of frontality and rotation there is another aspect to this museum which is totally absent in the Hejduk project. This aspect, which one can only call the "theme of erosion," is present in both the Eisenman and Graves projects, although the form in which it expresses itself differs from one to the other. Eisenman's feeling for erosion seems to be determined by his affiliation to the pre-war Italian Rationalist tradition. Eisenman's predilection for the "building as ruin" is not exploited for picturesque ends.[6] On the contrary, he appears to exploit the notion of the "building as ruin" from a "mythical" point of view.[7] For example, the timber boarded pattern of the ground floor suggests, with great precision, the presence of the "absence" of a support which has been magically removed. On this level the "build-

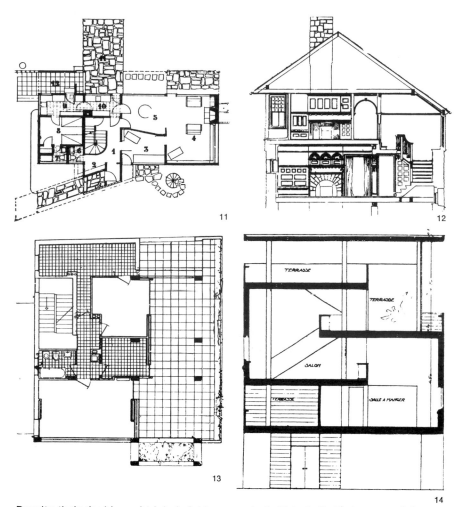

Despite their double and triple height spaces both Meier's Smith house and Graves Hanselmann house display affinities to Walter Gropius' own house of 1938 (fig: 11) designed with Marcel Breuer. A romantic concern with inflected views over and through the landscape is present in all three houses. Unconsciously these works, like the Gwathmey house, seem to recall something of the architectonic of the American shingle-style home of the late 80's (fig: 12). Their spatial ethos is ultimately as foreign to the interlocking spatial stereometry of Le Corbusier's Carthage Villa of 1928 (fig: 14) as it is to the monumental historicism of the Carminati and Terragni, Casa del Fascio at Lissone of 1939 (fig: 15).

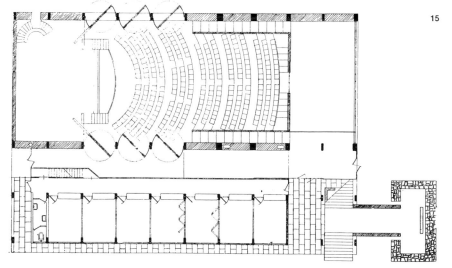

vertical slots are not used in re-entrant corners to separate two meeting planes. By the same token, structural frames are not used in this house to establish spatial layerings. This house could very easily be a load-bearing masonary structure, although it is in fact a load-bearing frame.

In all these houses rather tenuous "route" relationships are established between the building and the site. In all with exception of the Gwathmey and Hejduk houses there is an unresolved conflict between frontalization and rotation. Again in the Graves and Meier houses and in the Eisenman pavilion there is also an "erosion" of the surface, or of the structure, or of the mass, or of all three. Something of the general scaleness in these works suggests that they are "models" for larger buildings although I do not think this applies to either the Meier House in Darien or to the Gwathmey House on Long Island. Most of these houses with the exception of the Gwathmey residence appear to be indifferent to the general building culture. They are more concerned with a "cult of form." Despite this, most of these works are inescapably related to the East Coast tradition of light framed buildings (like the early United States houses of Gropius and Breuer, for example). In all these projects except Hejduk's there is an allusion to concrete forms and to so called "post-Corbusian" space; that is, there are certain syntactical references to Le Corbusier and hence a direct allusion to building in concrete.[7] Yet most of these structures are built in wood.

In the case of the Gwathmey house, the fact that the siding is left natural, places it well within an American wood building tradition. One cannot but be reminded of those remarkable bath houses designed by Muschenheim and built on Long Island in the late 30's. Are we in the presence here of a special East Coast subculture compounded of European abstraction and American technique? The degree of "intellectuality" present in these projects certainly varies. The Eisenman pavilion no doubt comprises the most complex system and at the same time it no doubt represents the most "mannered" of all these works. It is also patently far removed from any kind of American building culture of local origin. Nothing could be further from the Shingle Style than it is. Its affiliations are with Italy or, more precisely, with the Italian Rationalist movement of the 30's.

Finally, although all of these works are permeated by the aura of post-Corbusian space, none of them manipulate space in a way that at all resembles the work of Le Corbusier, as for example, at the Maison Cook where space is typically handled as though it were translucent mass. Maison Cook comprises a complex interlocking of blocks of space in which a fugal, mass-volume relationship is to be experienced by passing through and around the means of vertical access. I think there are few buildings here that even attempt such a proposition. Paradoxically only the Gwathmey House contains that necessary element of surprise that naturally accrues to such spatial transpositions.

1. This is a revised version of a text that was presented at a CASE meeting held at the Museum of Modern Art on May 9th and 10th, 1969. On this occasion the author gave it as a comparative critique of the five works exhibited at the meeting, namely, the Barenholtz Museum, Princeton, New Jersey, by Peter Eisenman; a House at Fort Wayne, Indiana, by Michael Graves; a House at Darien, Connecticut, by Richard Meier; a project for a Horizontal House by John Hejduk; and a house and studio designed by Charles Gwathmey. This criticism served to initiate discussion at that time.

2. A number of these architects have since started to work on larger commissions. An inflation of scale in the small domestic house is, of course, to be found throughout the modern movement. It is very prevalent, for example, in the West Coast work of R. M. Schindler.

3. This common base, of course, depends on a great deal more than either mutual friendship or team work. It is obvious that all these designers are, in varying degrees, subject to the influence of the work of Le Corbusier. Of more immediate critical import to the work shown at the CASE Meeting of 1969 was the Colin Rowe and Robert Slutzky article "Transparency: Literal and Phenomenal," published in *Perspecta No: 8* pp. 45–46.

4. The architect John Hejduk and the painter Robert Slutzky staged a joint architecture and painting show on the theme of the Diamond and the Square at the Architectural League in the Fall of 1967. This must surely go down as a largely unacknowledged exhibition of considerable import. The Dutch De Stijl movement exercised a particular influence of Hejduk's work at this time. Clearly a painting like Mondrian's *Foxtrot* influenced the development of Hejduk's *Project A: House* of 1967.

5. This is rather a loose comparison. The Casa Giuliani-Frigerio built at Como to the designs of Giuseppe Terragni in 1940 is approached along an east-west street and entered abruptly from the north. Where Le Corbusier's Villa Garches, for example, insists on distant frontal appraisal, Giuliani-Frigerio is eminently a block that has to be seen obliquely, from close proximity.

6. The "building as ruin" is a picturesque notion certainly dating in Western Architecture from Piranesi onwards. There is a flavor of such picturesqueness latent in the works of the Italian Rationalists due largely, I suspect, to the historicist-nationalist climate engendered by the Fascists. Typical of such an uneasy compound is the Casa del Fascio built at Lissone in 1939. This building designed by Anthonio Carminati and Giuseppe Terragni clearly divides between the "rationalist" main block and the historicist "tower of order," executed in stone to one side.

7. Despite the architect's disclaimer to the conrary, I tended to read the distortions to the inner columnar structure of the Barenholtz pavilion in mythical terms. What I vaguely intend by the term "myth" here has been best explained by Ernst Cassirer in his book *Myth and Language* when he wrote; "Language and Myth stand in an original and indissoluble correlation with one another, from which they both emerge but gradually as independent elements. They are two diverse shoots from the same parent stem, the same impulse of symbolic formulation, springing from the same basic mental activity, a concentration and heightening of simple sensory experience."

# Peter Eisenman

## House I  1967

Cardboard Architecture: House I
Peter D. Eisenman

These two articles by Peter D. Eisenman, "House I" and "House II" were first drafted in November of 1969 and April of 1970, respectively. In both cases they were redrafted and necessarily condensed for publication in the first edition of this book.

In this edition the substance of the ideas remain the same as in the first publication. The only intention in the changes which have been made here has been to clarify their content.

At present most buildings are burdened by their very description as "museums" or "country houses" with a weight of cultural meaning which is here meant to be neutralized by the opposition of an equally loaded term. "Cardboard," usually a derogatory term in architectural discussion (as Baroque and Gothic were when first used), is used here deliberately as an ironic and pre-emptory symbol for my argument.

Cardboard is used to question the nature of our perception of reality and thus the meanings ascribed to reality. Thus it is not so much a metaphor describing the forms of the building but rather its intention. For example, models are often made of cardboard, so the term raises the question of the form in relation to the process of design: is this a building or is it a model?

Cardboard is used to shift the focus from our existing conception of form in an aesthetic and functional context to a consideration of form as a marking or notational system. The use of cardboard attempts to distinguish an aspect of these forms which are designed to act as a signal or a message and at the same time the representation of them as a message.

Cardboard is used to signify the result of the particular way of generating and transforming a series of primitive integer relationships into a more complex set of specific relationships which become the actual building. In this sense cardboard is used to denote the particular deployment of columns, walls, and beams as they define space in a series of thin planar, vertical layers. It is not so much a literal recognition of the actual surfaces as cardboardlike and thus insubstantial but rather is meant to signify the virtual or implied layering which is produced by the particular configuration.

In this context House I and House II are experiments which attempt to translate these concepts into a possible working method and into a physical environment.

There is often an attempt made to rationalize architecture in terms of its program. In a paper given at the R.I.B.A. in 1957, Sir John Summerson represented this position quite explicitly when he attempted to make a case for a theory of architecture with such a programmatic basis. In essence, Summerson said the source of unity in modern architecture is in the social sphere, in other words, in the architect's program. But it would seem that the situation is more complicated than Summerson allowed. For if the program is to sustain such an emphasis, it should be able to specify and distinguish what the facts of a particular situation are, and except for certain physical laws, facts in a programmatic sense are in reality a series of value judgements. Much of the oeuvre of modern architectural theory is involved in a basic dilemma precisely because it has refused to distinguish between problems of fact and problems of value. And more specifically, because it has refused to recognize problems of form as predicated by anything except ideas of social and technological change or as a matter for stylistic and aesthetic speculation.

A museum as a program offers very little in the way of specific functional requirements which can act as either a suggestion for or limitation to a formal development. This might account for the fact that many of the best museums are ones which have been created in buildings originally designed for other purposes. Equally, since it is difficult to define a precise form from the functional requirements, the form of a museum is often realized as a very idealized shape. Since very little is imposed on the form of a museum by its function, its form may be used to help clarify part of the problem outlined above.

The making of form can, for instance, be considered as a problem of logical consistency; as a consequence of the logical structure inherent in any formal relationship. The making of form in this sense is more than the satisfaction of functional requirements and more than the creation of aesthetically pleasing objects, but rather the exposition of a set of formal relationships.

House I was an attempt to conceive of and understand the physical environment in a logically consistent manner, potentially independent of its function and its meaning.

The thesis presented in House I, the Barenholtz Pavilion, is as follows: one way of producing an environment which can accept or give a more precise and richer meaning than at present, is to understand the nature of the structure of form itself, as opposed to the relationship of form to function or of form to meaning.

House I posits one alternative to existing conceptions of spatial organization. Here there was an attempt, first, to find ways in which form and space could be structured so that they would produce a set of formal relationships which is the result of the inherent logic in the forms themselves, and, second, to control precisely the logical relationships of forms.

There were three steps in this process in House I. First, an attempt was made to make a distinction between those aspects of form which respond to programmatic and technological requirements and those aspects of form which relate to a logical structure. In order to make this distinction, an attempt was made to reduce or unload the existing meaning of the forms. Second, a formal structure was made from these marks in the actual environment. Third, this formal structure of marks was related to another formal structure of a more abstract and fundamental nature. The purpose of this procedure was to provide an awareness of formal information latent in any environment which previously was unavailable to the individual.

One aspect of the first step was an attempt to reduce or unload the existing meaning of the forms dictated by function so that the forms could be seen as a series of primitive marks. This was attempted through a manipulation of the relationship of the color, texture, and shape of the built forms. White forms are used in House I to shift our visual perception and conception of such forms; from the perception of a real, tangible, white volumetric architecture to the conception of an abstract, colored planar space; from the polemic of the "white" of the 1920's to the neutrality of "cardboard." The white color and the flat texture are closer to an abstract plane than say a natural wood or a cut stone wall. Also the very fact that the white planes carry a specific meaning related to a known style (the International Style), makes them less likely to take on new meaning. It should even be easier to reduce their existing meaning, as will be seen below, when they are placed in a different context. To this end, color and material will be seen in the argument below to be used in House I as "marking" devices. Traditionally, when white was used, window mullions and hand rails were painted black, and planes of primary or pastel colors were introduced for aesthetic effect. In House I, white or black planes are used simply as opposites in a formal structure while grey or clear glass are considered as neutral.

A second aspect of the initial marking process involved the structural elements — the columns and beams. They appear initially to be rather conventional parts of a structural system. However, upon closer inspection this is found not to be the case. It is actually not possible to determine how the structure functions from looking at the columns and beams. All of the apparent structural apparatus — the exposed beams, the free standing columns — are in fact non-structural. When this is understood, a first step has been taken to unload, albeit in a very primitive way, their structural meaning. While the apparent physical fact is the same whether they are load-bearing or not, their meaning has changed because they are in fact not load-bearing, and thus the intention implied in their use in a particular location must now be considered in a different way. Once one has understood that they are not structural one must ask what are they? Why are they where they are? Take them away, or change their shape, and what have you got?

It can also be asked, why go to all this trouble? If the columns are supposed to be non-structural, why not just cut them off at the top so that we know immediately by the fact that they do not continue to the ceiling that they are not columns but merely a notation for some other purpose? But cutting the columns short of the ceiling would in fact do the opposite of what is intended. It would give the column a further meaning by obviously calling attention to itself as a non-supporting column, whereas it is supposed to be merely one mark or a primitive element in a formal scheme.

The second intention of this work called for taking these marks and deploying them in such a way so as to make a complete formal structure and to show that this struc-

ture was a primary consideration in the design of the whole building. To focus on this, required a further shift in the primary conception of an environment; this time from a concern merely for marking elements and their meaning to a concern for their relationship in a formal structure. To force this shift in House I, the formal structure was in a sense over-stressed or over-articulated so that it would become a dominant aspect of the building. One means to over-stress such a structure was to suggest two simultaneous structures which overlay and interact. These were based on a simple combination of two pairs of formal references: planes and volumes, on the one hand; frontal and oblique relationships, on the other.

The two formal structures are marked by the columns and beams. These are not deployed in a regular pattern such as a columnar grid, which in such a condition could be seen as a neutral referent, nor are they to be seen as the residue of such a grid, but rather they are intentionally placed in an apparently random order. This intention can be explained in the following way. In the first instance, the space is conceived of as a layering or plaiding (cross layering) of planes. The rectilinear columns and beams are placed so that they will read as a residue of these planes. Conversely, the round columns are used to mark the intersections of two planes, which might possibly be read as joined at this intersection, thus forming volumes if the columns were square. The round column prevents the possible interpretation of columns as residual "corners" of volumes. In the second instance, the three columns (a fourth is marked in the floor), because of their particular disposition, also mark a diagonal system. They can be interpreted in the following way. If both pairs of round columns and beams were seen to span the entire space (Fig. 5) they would read, despite the roundness of the columns, as part of the frontal layering. By taking away two columns, a round one in the space and one attached to the wall (Fig. 6) as well as the portions of the beams connecting to these columns, an implied diagonal is created.

Thus the intention was to use the columns and beams to mark two systems without giving preference to either. Together the counterpoint of these two formal systems, the frontal planar layering and the diagonal volumetric shift, overlaid and interacting with one another make it more difficult to read a

single coherent formal system directly from the physical fact. Rather they reinforce the intention that these marks in order to be understood first require disengagement of the two systems from one another, an activity which takes place in the mind.

Such a marking of formal relationships, in the actual environment, has usually been the extent of the architect's concern with formal systems. But the present work takes one further step. If we analyze the nature of meaning in any specific context we realize it has two aspects. The first is meaning which is iconographic and symbolic and derives from the relation of the form to some reference which is external to it. For example, the particular juxtaposition of solids, columns, windows, and railings in Le Corbusier's Villa Savoye is intended as a direct recall of the super-structure of the modern ocean liners, and with it all the implications of the sea: discovery, newness, and ultimately man's conquest of nature. But underlying that level of meaning there is another aspect, itself a potential source of information, which conditions any iconographic interpretation; it is derived from, and is in a sense inherent in the structure of the form. For example, the same juxtaposition of solids, voids, and columns at Poissy gives us cues to entry, sequence of movement, the relationship of open to closed space, of the center to the perimeter, and so forth. This information can be said to be the product of the internal structure of form itself. While formal relationships can exist in an environment at a real, actual level, where an individual is aware of them through his senses — perception, hearing, touching — they can also exist at another level in which though not seen, they can be known. This second level is inherent in any environment and is used by an individual whether or not he is aware of it. This second level conditions the way we perceive the first level by providing a structure for the visual cues which exist in the first level. And since it has the capacity to be known, we must be concerned with how this happens. If we mark both these levels in the environment they can be explicitly perceived and understood. This is the third aspect of the work — a shift in focus from an actual structure to an implied structure and to the relationship between the two.

This second level may be thought of as a range of abstract and more universal formal regularities which exist in any conception of physical space. These formal regularities are universal in the sense that such formal concepts as solid and void, centroidal and linear, planar and volumetric are primitive notions which cannot be reduced and which exist in a state of opposition in any spatial conception. This second level includes in addition to a set of irreducible formal regularities, the transformations of these regularities necessary to produce a specific environment. Transformations may be described by such formal actions as shear, compression, and rotation, to produce a new level of formal information in any specific physical environment. Again the marking is used to signal the interaction between these two levels. The physical environment can then be seen not only in its functional and iconographic dimensions but also in its formal one — as being generated from a series of abstract formal regularities which may be described as a deep structure. These transformations and regularities have no substantial existence but are merely a description of this second level of formal relationships, in other words, a possible model for an architectural deep structure.

One means of making the deep structure in a particular environment explicit is to force an individual to experience the environment as a notational system which has a recognizable relationship to a deep structure. This is attempted in House I in the following manner. First, the series of formal relationships which are marked in the actual space (the parallel layers and diagonal volumes) create a contrast between actual space and implied space. This contrast makes one initially aware of the presence of another level of formal structure. Second, the two sets of formal notations which are discernible (one read as incomplete, the other asymmetrical) because one can conceive of a symmetrical and complete structure of formal regularities, are super-imposed. These notations which are variations of the formula ABABA appear in the actual environment in the following way. The first of these corresponds to the formula $A_1B_1A_1A_1$ (Fig. 3) and the second to the formula $A_2B_1A_1B_2A_2$ (Fig. 4); the middle terms $B_1A_1$ being common to both. When they are overlaid on one another, the underlying structure is seen as compressed, but when they are slipped apart in the mind, it reveals itself to be a simple symmetrical structure.

The basis for creating this relationship of actual structure to deep structure is quite primitive. It depends on an initial shift along a diagonal to create two implied square volumes (Figs. 1 and 2). One square may be seen as shifted out of the other or vice versa so that the notations both for the plaid frontal layering and for the diagonal volumes can be seen as deriving from one, more basic system. The diagonal is read as a resolution of the two directions in the plaid, or the plaid is read as the result of the diagonal shift. Thus the deep structure is revealed only through an embedded relationship between two formal structures in the actual environment. Although one may perceive these two structures in the actual environment, one is unable to perceive the deep structure because of its existence in the environment as an irregular gestalt. These actual structures thus have a common relationship in a deep structure which is not perceptible but which can be understood after both structures have been perceived.

Any physical environment has this second or deep structural level, which not only has the capacity to convey information but does so continually at a less-than-conscious level. It exists without being consciously designed, and there is a conceptual capacity within each individual to receive this information. Marking the deep structure in the actual environment may bring it to a more conscious level. As was said above, there is no reason or meaning intended in the use of this particular formal strategy. The two overlaid systems are neither good nor bad in themselves. They are intended merely to exemplify the logic inherent in any formal structure, and the potential capacity of that logic to provide an area of new meaning.

In summary, three shifts were attempted in House I. Each concerned an attempt to separate the actual physical environment from its traditional relationship to function and meaning, to neutralize the influence of these on the viewer. The first concerned the marking of the elements of the actual environment; the second concerned the marking of the formal structure in the actual environment; the third concerned the marking of the relationship of this formal structure to a deep structure.

Such a conception of design attempts to change the primary intention of architectural form from the perception of space to understanding the relationship of marks in that space to what is called here a deep structure. The capacity to understand, as op-

posed to experience this intention does not depend entirely on the observer's particular cultural background, his subjective perceptions, or his particular mood at any given time, all of which condition his usual experience of an actual environment, but rather it depends on his innate capacity to understand formal structures.

Such a position introduces, as a primary concern of architecture, the use of physical form as a marking to produce, as it were, a new mental image of an environment different from that which we are actually seeing. The deep structure, when it is combined with the perceptible physical reality, has the potential, if it is structured in a precise fashion, to make available a new level of information. The more this structure approximates a purely formal environment, the less traditional the meaning it possesses, and thus the closer it is to an environment that might be a vehicle for such new information.

To do this, form must be first considered to be potentially separable from its existing perception and conception, and second, it must be considered as capable of changing or raising the level of consciousness by proposing a critique of the existing situation in architecture.

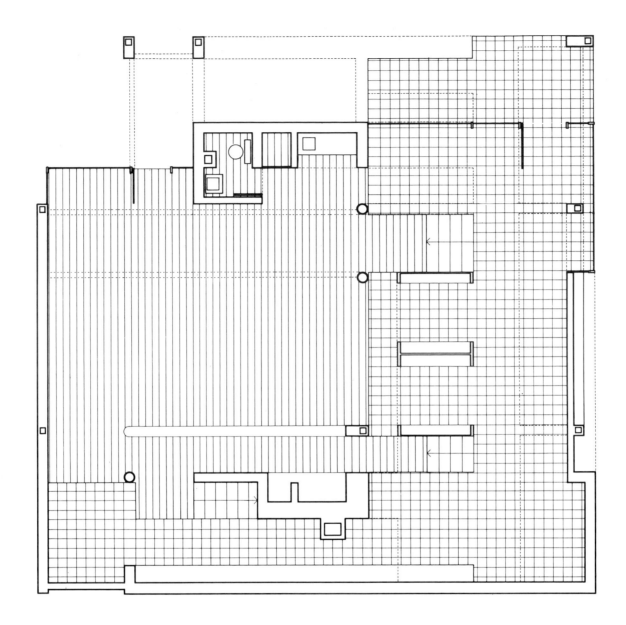

Lower Level Plan

West Elevation

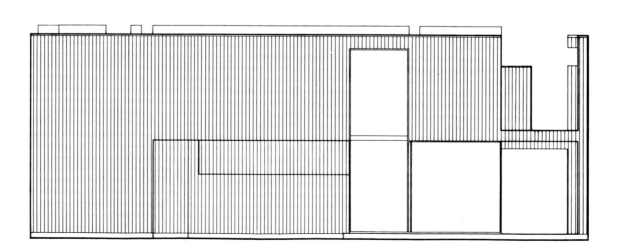

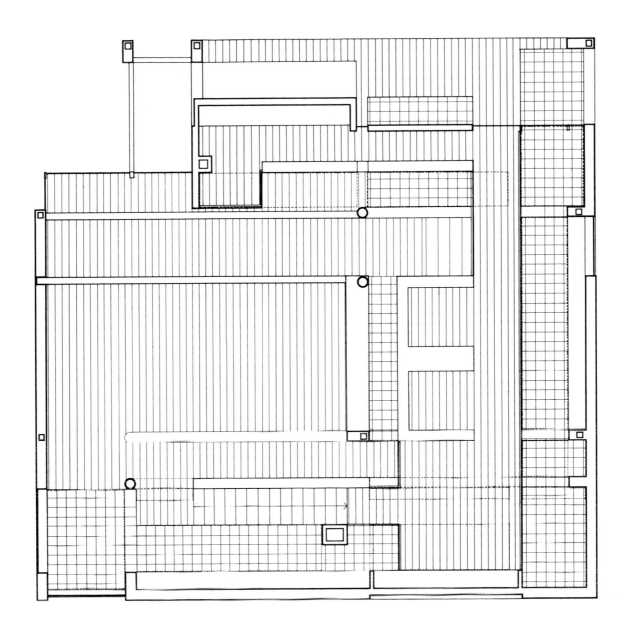

Upper Level Plan

0                    5

Section

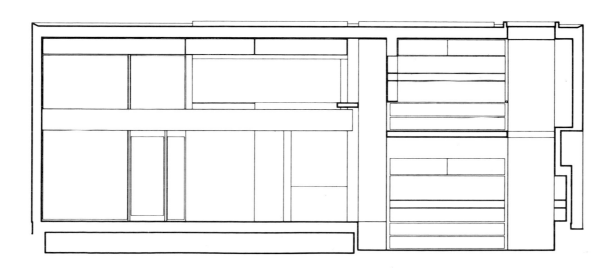

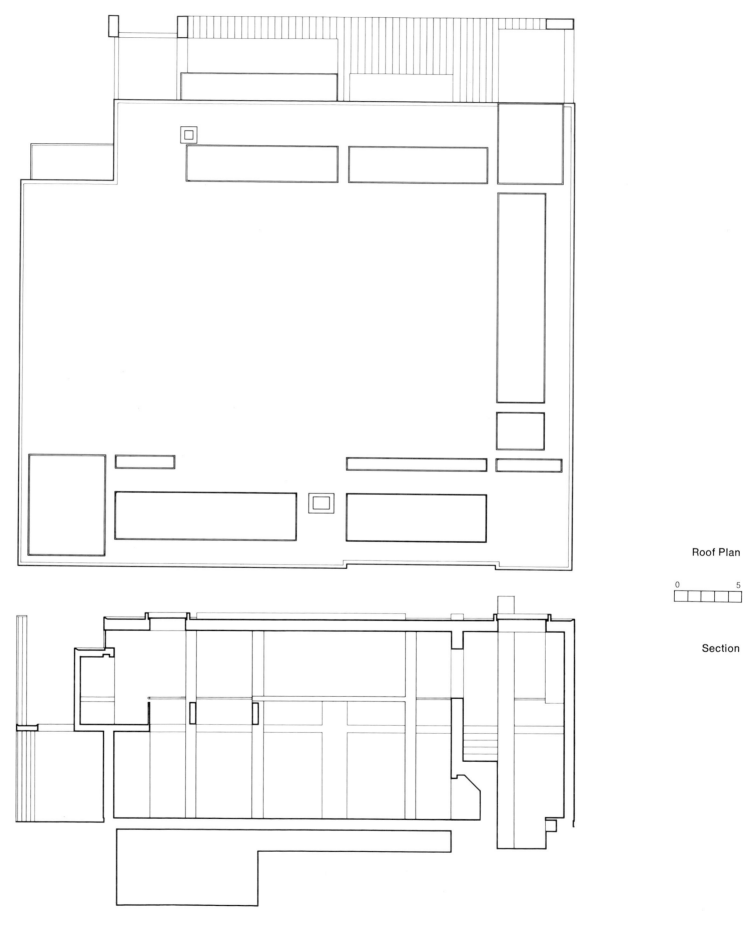

Roof Plan

0                    5

Section

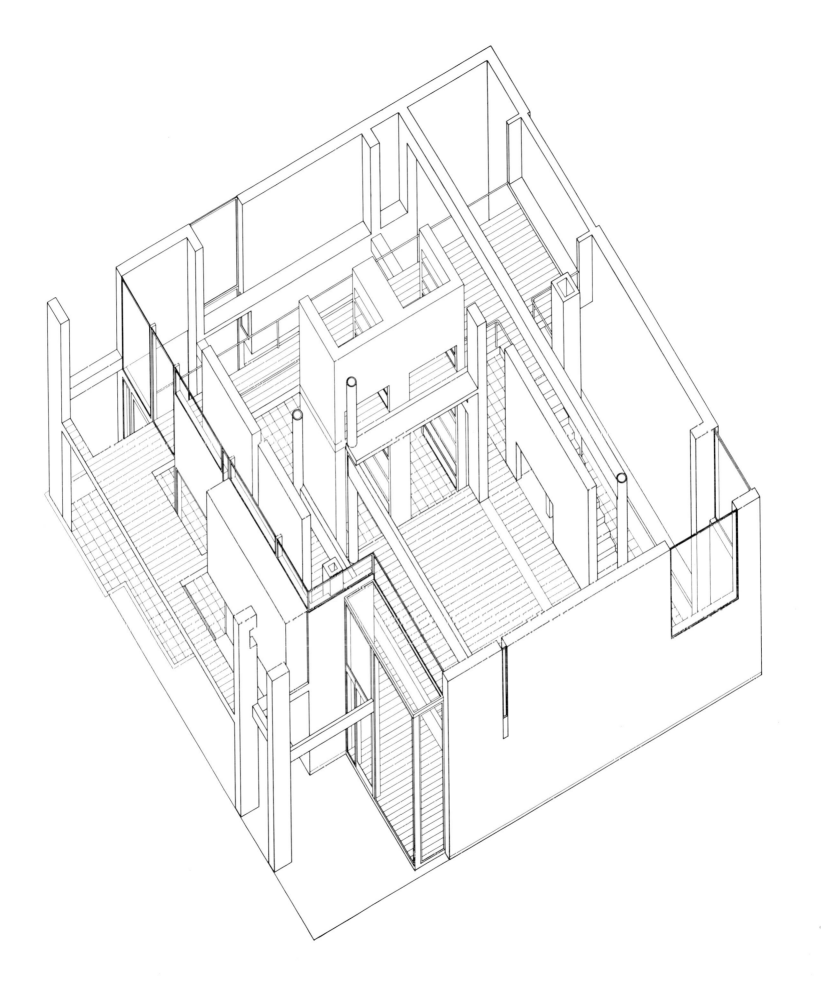

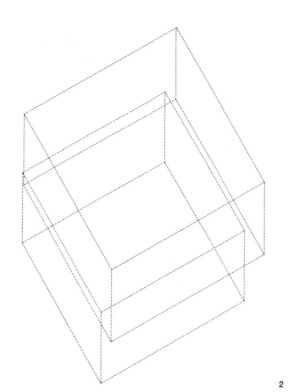

1

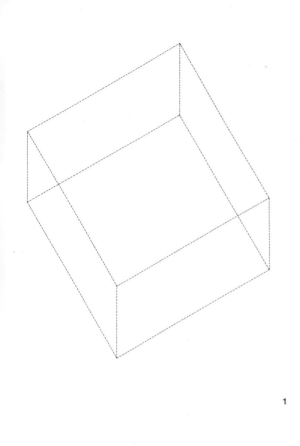

2

a₁ a₁

b₁

a₁

3

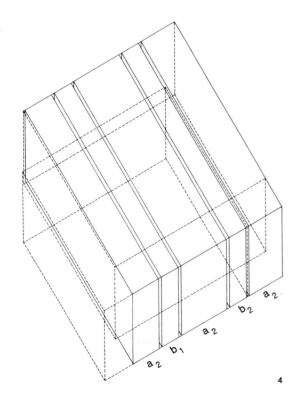

a₂ b₁

a₂

b₂ a₂

4

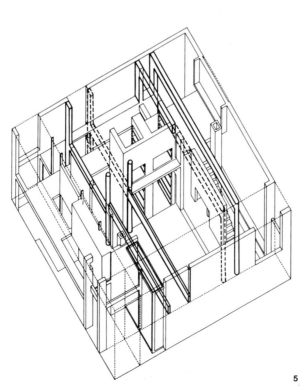

5

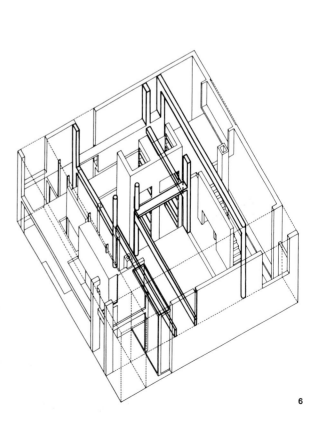

6

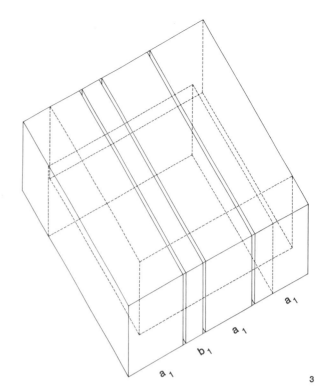

# Peter Eisenman

## House II 1969

Cardboard Architecture: House II
Peter D. Eisenman

In the past, even when limited by the constraints posed by available materials, architects sought to use structural elements in ways other than those dictated by purely functional requirements. Modern technology provided architecture with new means of conceiving of space. In a sense, space was no longer necessarily limited or defined by structure. It was possible to examine such elements as the column and wall as other than the resolution of functional problems. This was especially true with respect to the use of the load-bearing wall; the column became a primary structural element and along with the non-load-bearing wall, a potentially innovative formal device.

House I was concerned with using columns and walls to mark a set of formal relationships. Continuing from this, House II is concerned with a systematic development of two ways in which information may be conceived of and derived from the interaction of formal relationships.

To articulate these ways of conceiving and producing formal information in House II, certain formal means were chosen each involving an overloading of the object with formal references.

This development can be seen first from a set of analytic diagrams (Figs. 1–15). These diagrams describe the development of a set of abstract formal propositions as a possible condition of an underlying structure and their initial transformation into a specific environment.

Any given coordinates of space can be described as either linear, planar, or volumetric. The coordinates of a cubic space are described by its edge or its center; the edge composed of lines or planes, the center by a line or a volume. In this particular house the center condition is arbitrarily defined by a square volume. From this the original square is divided into nine squares. These squares are marked by a matrix of 16 square columns. The first six diagrams present one

set of conditions possible from this initial definition. The selection of the conditions as opposed to any other condition of such a deep structure is at this stage of work, arbitrary. Figure 2 shows the gridded nine square arrangement. Figures 3, 4, and 5 select and isolate three possible conditions of that gridding: as a matrix of 16 columns, as a series of four planes, or as a series of three volumes seen as solids between the planes. It is to be noted that the planar and volumetric conditions are linear and directional in opposing axes. While there are obviously other combinations of planes and volumes, these chosen oppositions suggest one prior condition of an underlying structure which when transformed will produce a level of implied or virtual information in the actual space. Thus while the grid of nine squares can be seen as an underlying structure, the axial opposition of planes and volumes will be seen to create a transformation of this structure. The assumption here is that these initial spatial oppostions in some way permit the articulation of a virtual relatlonship between the actual environment and underlying structure. (How or why this happens is a subject for future work.)

The further diagrams concern the development of one possible transformation, from this underlying structure to an actual environment. There was a second transformatlon following from the Initial deployment of lines, planes, and volumes which was a dislocation, in the form of a diagonal shift. (This can also be seen in the dotted outline of two bounding volumes in Fig. 2–6.) This shift created the potential for developing another set of oppositions in the actual environment by articulating two squares, one defined by the planes and the second defined by the matrix of columns. The particular location of columns, walls, and volumes produced by the diagonal shift creates two datum references. It is possible to read the shear walls as a neutral referent especially when seen from the north, whereupon the columns can be read as the residue of these planes, transposed diagonally from them (Fig. 9). Alternatively, the columns can be read as a neutral referent, especially when seen from the south, whereupon the shear walls may be read as having been shifted from the plane

of the columns. The column grid also acts as a neutral referent for a second set of formal readings involving a diagonal cross-layering. One diagonal is articulated by the volumes of the upper level, which step up and back from left to right. This movement crosses at right angles the diagonal established by the shear walls (Fig. 10), which repeat and reduce in length as they move along the diagonal from the full-length shear wall at the north. Because of this diagonal shift, the implied planes formed by the columns and beams cut through the volumes in such a way as to create a condition in space where the actual space can be read as layered. The layering produces an opposition between the actual geometry and an implied geometry; between real space which is negative or void and implied volume which is positive or solid. This can be seen in Figs. 11–15. This layering also produces a plaiding in both axes. Implied solid volumes can now be read on either side of the original column datum. The residual volumes are further articulated by the location of the roof skylights which are placed directly over them in the north–south axis. (Fig. 16)

Other ways were explored to create a dialectic or an opposition between an actual relationship and an implied relationship in the environment using the column and the wall, and the wall and the volume. First the columns, walls, and volumes were treated as equally weighted in terms of disposition and number, and second, they were seen as variants of one abstract planar system. In other words, through a formal device using the plane as a fulcrum, a dialectic was created between the real column, wall, and room volume, and that which is implied line, plane, and solid. In this context, a room volume is seen as an extension of the wall, while a column appears as a residue of the wall. The deliberate compression of the usually differentiated formal systems — the column system, the wall system, the window system — into an undifferentiated construct, reinforced a condition where it was difficult for these conventional architectural elements to be considered individually as objects; they became merely parts of a total structure of relationships. The focus is thus transferred from the physical object itself to

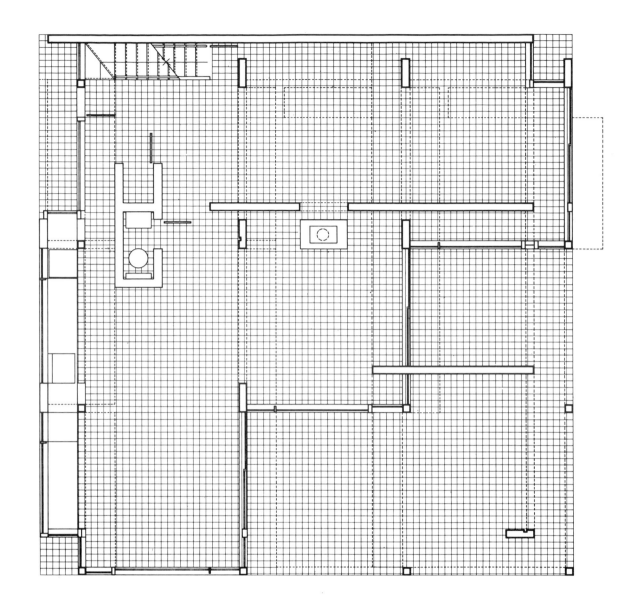

Lower Level Plan

South Elevation

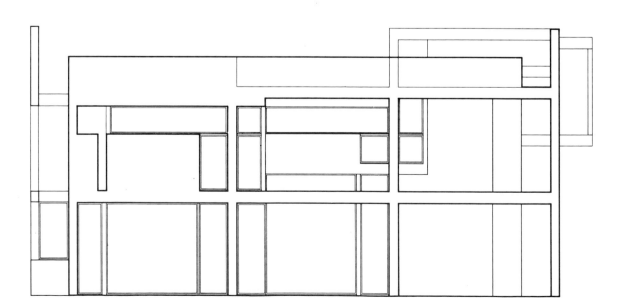

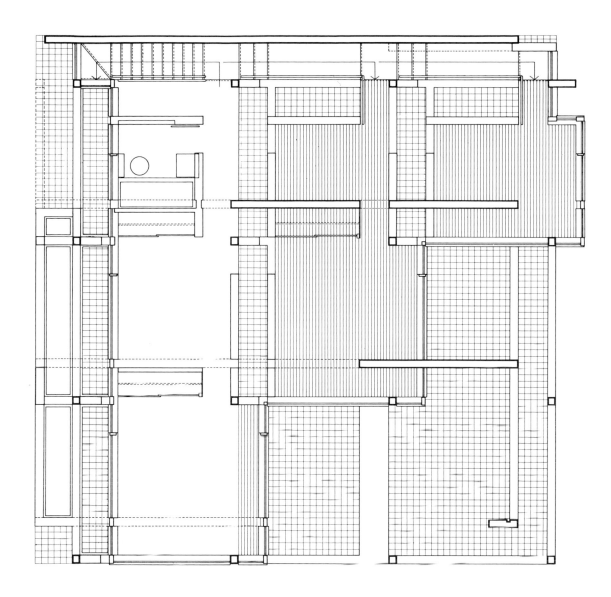

**Upper Level Plan**

0       5

**West Elevation**

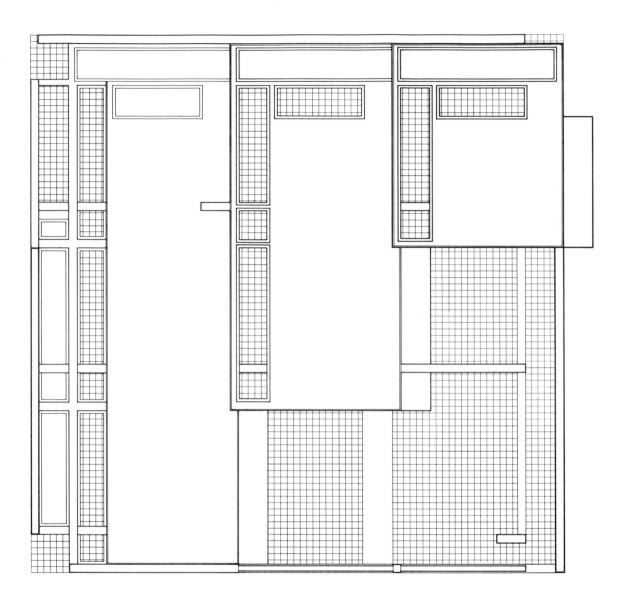

Roof Plan

0          5

Section

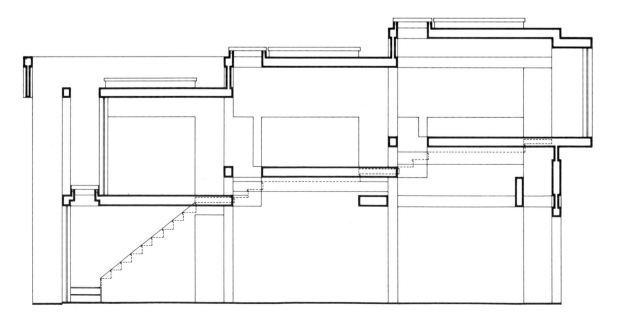

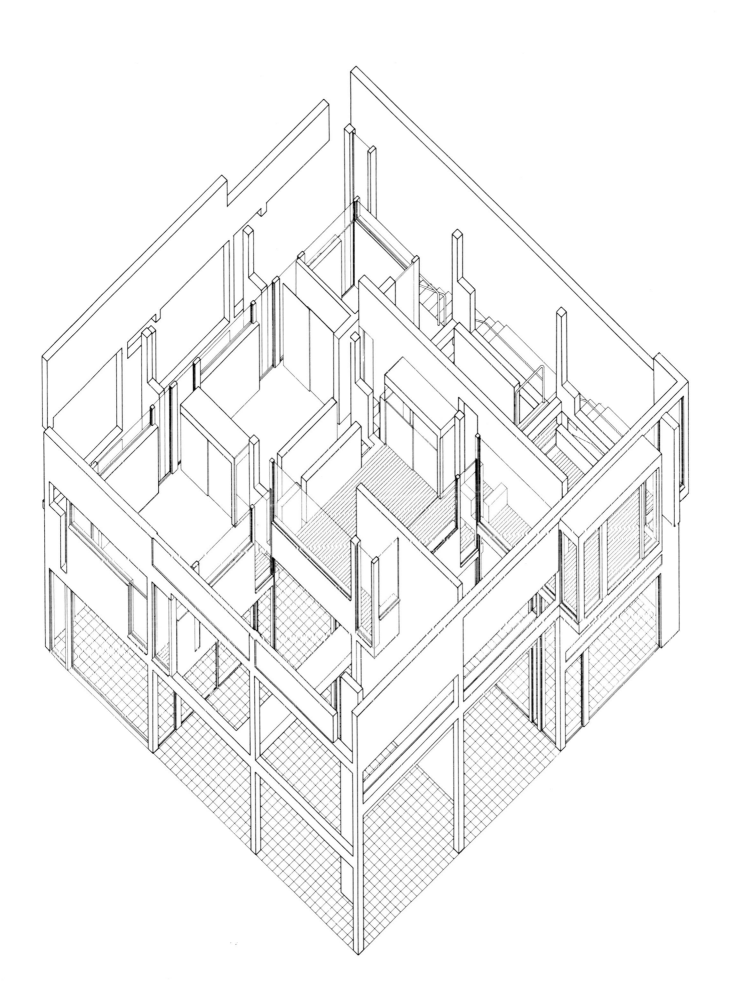

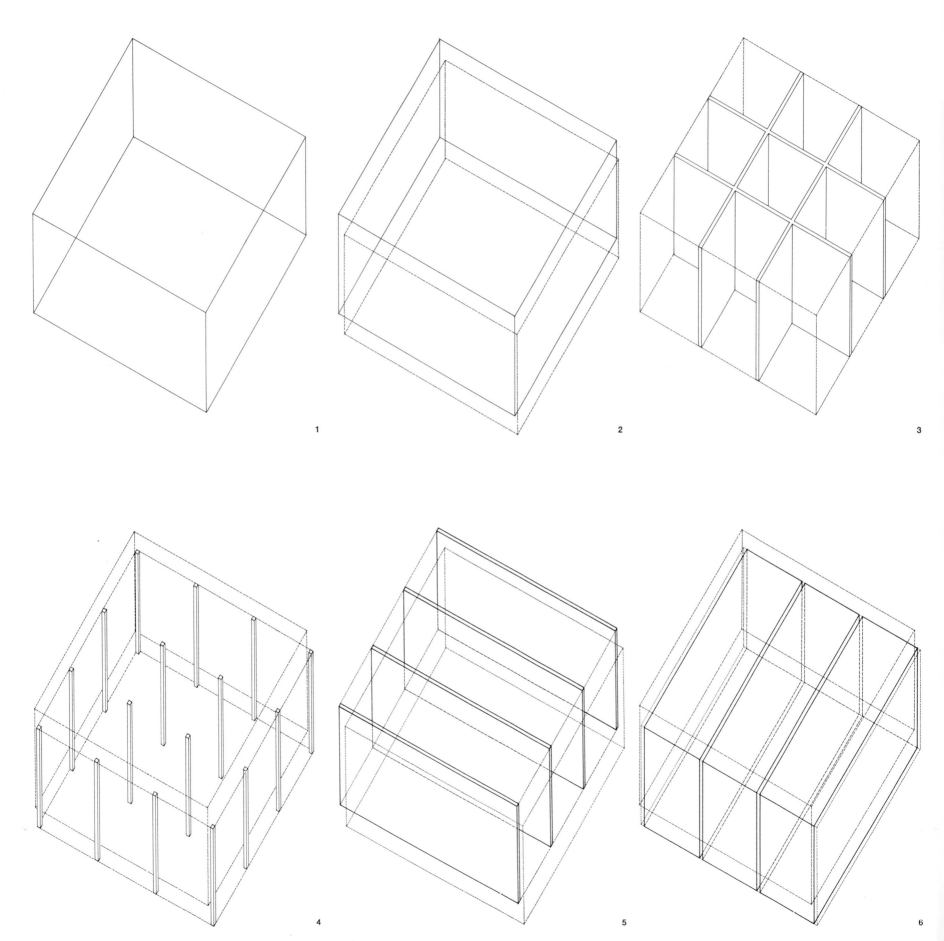

1

2

3

4

5

6

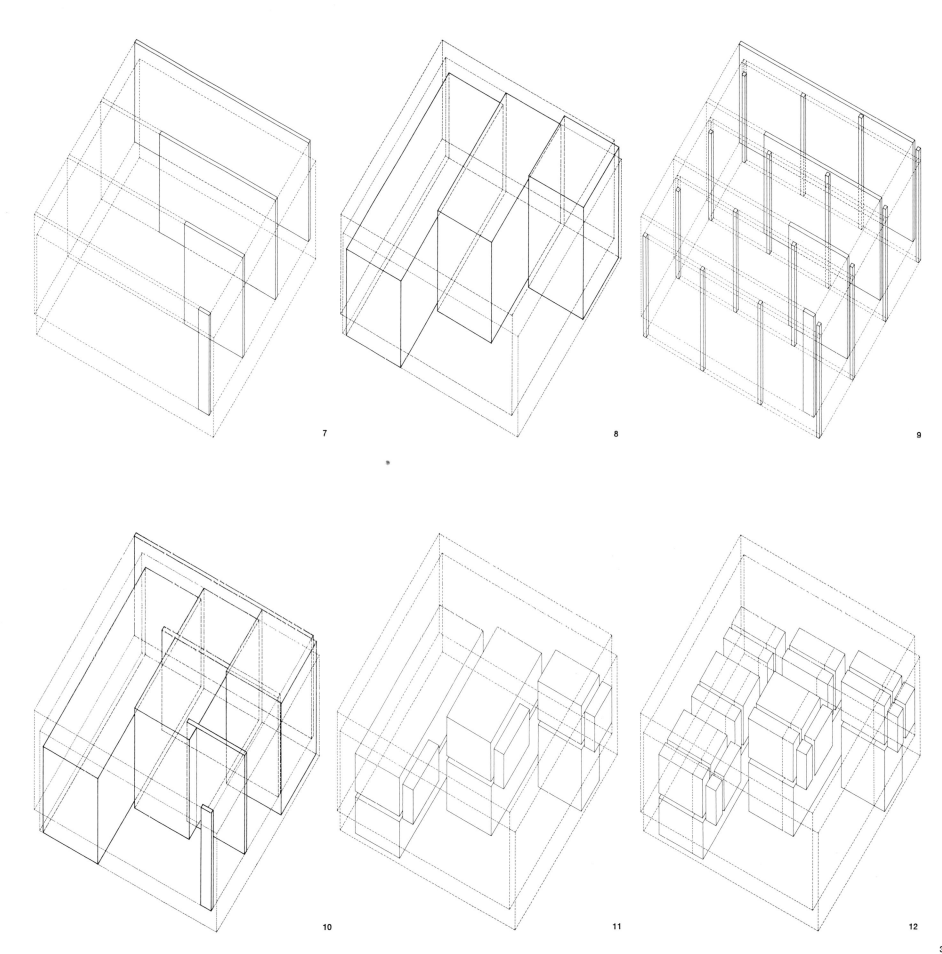

7

8

9

10

11

12

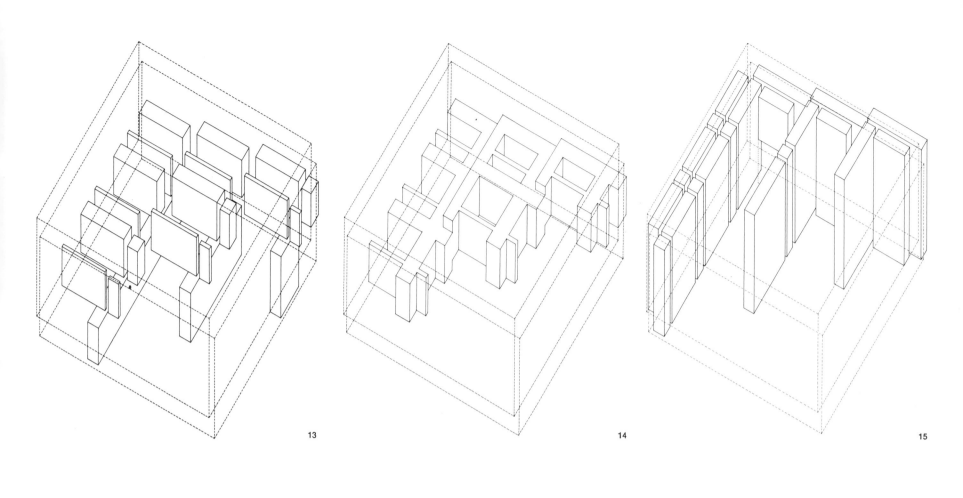

13    14    15

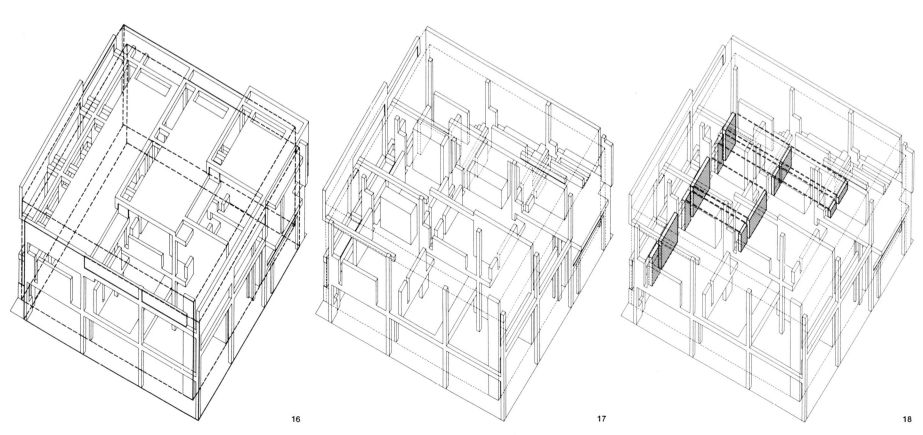

16    17    18

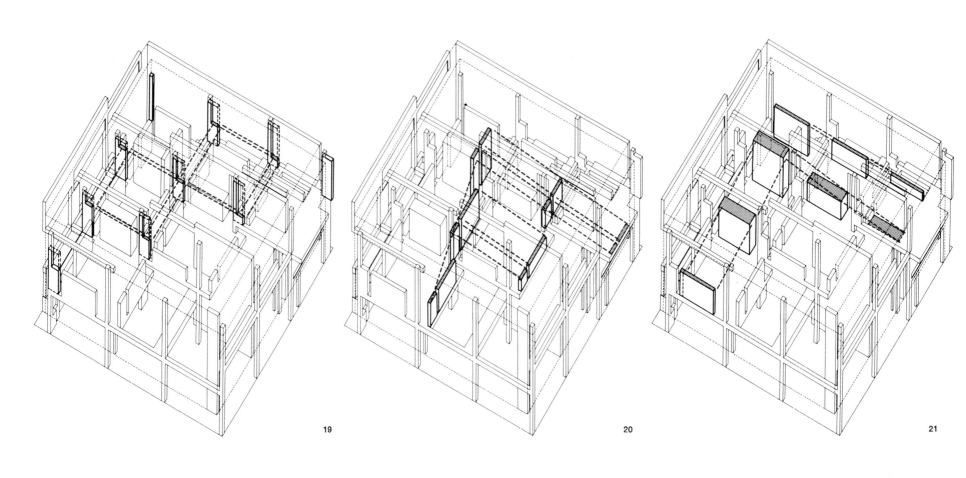

19  20  21

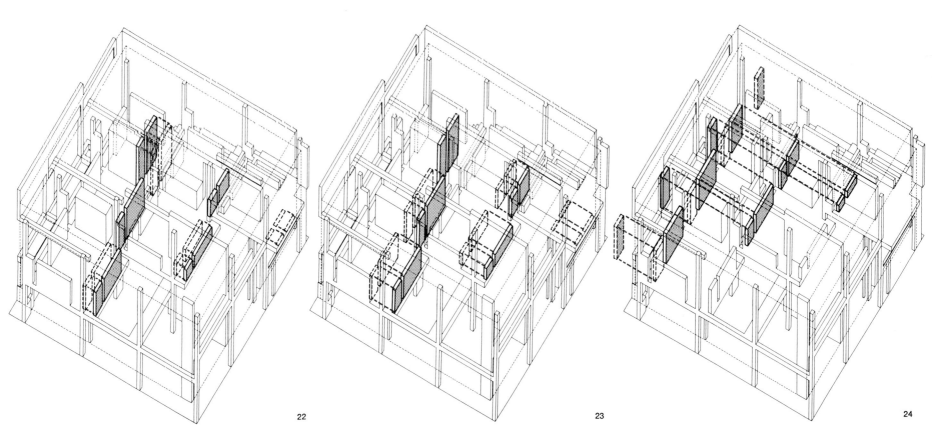

22  23  24

# Michael Graves

## Hanselmann House    1967

### Architecture as the World Again?
William La Riche

Placed in the midst of chaotic nature, man for his own security creates and surrounds himself with a zone of protection in harmony with what he is and what he thinks; he needs things whose existence he has himself determined. The things he makes for himself are a creation which contrasts all the more with his natural surroundings because its aim is closer to his mind, and further away and more detached from his body. We can say that the further human creations are from our immediate grasp, the more they tend to pure geometry; a violin or a chair, things which come into close contact with the body, are of a less pure geometry; but a town is pure geometry. It is then that he achieves what we call order.

—Le Corbusier[1]

Le Corbusier chooses examples to illustrate his point which are in some ways insupportable. And yet, the central observation is profound: the continuum between particularity and generality in design often is congruent with the gradations of scale. Other distinctions may be generated from this premise—distinctions between object and framework, actual and ideal. Architecture may be seen as 'intermediary'[2] form, existing as object and framework and yet between those two states. Mies van der Rohe's museum in Berlin (figure 1) presents the ambiguity of this condition with instructive (if literal) clarity: the upper gallery is a precisely delimited object within the framework of the city's streets; it is a framework, in turn (with the gridding of its columnar organization, coffered ceiling, and lighting layout), to the objects it contains.

In painting, the concept of framework frequently is registered as what some critics call 'internal architecture.' Herbert Read credits Juan Gris with establishing the primacy over subject matter of that proportional geometry with which he organized each canvas in the initial stage of composition.[3] He asserts that, with Gris, "representational elements *might* afterwards be introduced to fill in the abstract design."[4] Certain leaders of the movement toward abstraction (according to Read) fixed on Gris' position and carried it one step further by establishing the architecture of the painting as not merely primary but sufficient in itself.[5]

What Read and other explicators of the Cubist achievement failed to see is precisely what the non-representational painters chose to ignore: Gris did not rely solely on the evocative power of geometry to determine his subject matter. Kahnweiler writes that Gris 'worshiped' Mallarmé.[6] The influence of the Symbolist poet on Gris' art and thought was crucial and pervasive. Gris shared Mallarmé's sense of the artist's quest for an unattainable ideal of purity. He followed, in addition, that poet's practice of selecting, organizing, and presenting subject matter in a way that expressed a set of metaphorical intentions. The significance of all those open windows, guitars, harlequins, and glaciers in Gris' paintings (figure 2) begins to become apparent after one has read such poems of Mallarmé as "les Fenêtres," "le Pître chatié," and "l'Azur." The continuing tensions and occasional syntheses of formal, representational, and metaphorical concerns invested Gris' work with a richness of meaning unique in Cubism.

And yet, it was mainly for the clarity of the internal architecture of his paintings that Le Corbusier called Gris the "strongest and most noble of the Cubist painters."[7] Passages from Gris' paintings occasionally reappeared in Le Corbusier's plans, but there is little evidence that it mattered to the architect whether it had been a mandolin or a compote which provided the shape he needed to complete some fragment of composition.

The architect, unlike the painter, traditionally has possessed the vocabulary from which to create symbolic statements without adopting a mimetic strategy toward natural or man-made phenomena. Le Corbusier, as is well-known, turned repeatedly to the engineering structures of an industrialized society for both aesthetic characteristics and specific images to employ in his designs. The 'concepts' he demanded that these characteristics and these images express, however, were seldom more elaborate than simplicity of form and clarity of construction. There were exceptions, to be sure, and they were notable: in the Villa Savoye major compositional themes supplemented the superficially perceptible similarities to ocean liners; the Unite d'Habitation incorporated, in addition, the ocean liner's irreducible, directly stated, and self-contained social organization. Le Corbusier seldom explored systematically the combination within a single composition of specifically referential, metaphoric statements (e.g., the column is a tree) with arche-

1

2

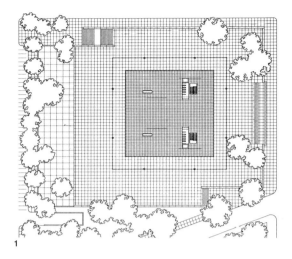

3

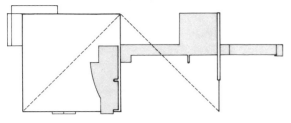

Hanselmann House

typal spatial organizations and experiences (e.g., the establishment of precincts of graduated sacrality, the procession through them). The architecture of Michael Graves embodies the most extensive and provocative recent exploration of these themes. Graves' Hanselmann Residence incorporates the geometric bias of Gris' art. If the accommodation of activity-type is a subject matter of architecture, then, in an initial reading, subject matter is definitely subordinated in this design to the geometric framework of a double cube. And yet, form and meaning are (as they were with Gris) mutually determining from the start.

The assertion of an idealized framework to delimit the house and its precinct reflects an attitude so persistent in man's history as to verge on the archetypal. The opposition of this Euclidean abstraction to the verdent specificity of a sloping site evokes images of Greek architecture—of, for example, the Marmaria near Delphi (figure 3). Here, the placement of an order so relentlessly 'reasoned' amid the localized tropisms of 'unreasoned' nature results in the enhancement through contrast of each of these two orders. In the Hanselmann Residence the site is less spectacular and the mathematics less insistent than at the Marmaria; still, the composition stands as further evidence that the continuity of opposition between object and framework obtains at several scales and can exist, even, between artifice and nature.

In a second classic opposition, the emphatic solidity of the house contrasts with the implied cubic void which separates it from the road: the building and the remainder of its precinct are endowed with a volumetric equivalence. That equivalence is indicated literally in plan by the presence of the double square. Graves finds it ironic that architects achieve the most precise registration of their compositional intentions in plan: in proceeding through a building only vertical planes perceived frontally can be seen with any objectivity; one's perception of horizontal planes is, of course, distorted by perspective. To establish a compositional intention in plan, then, is to establish it principally as an idea and only secondarily as a phenomenon.

In the Hanselmann Residence, the use of frontality is central to the architect's attempt to attain a perceptible lucidity of organization. Primary movement ocurs at 90° to the layered deployment of principal facades. The progression is from the general to the particular, from the undifferentiated and continuous space of the street to the highly differentiated, discontinuous interior spaces of the house itself. In accord with Le Corbusier's

4

proposition, moreover, there is a graduation in the formal complexity of the composition beginning at the street facade, where a pipe-rail frame verges on the immateriality of 'pure geometry.'

The organization of the Hanselmann design is intended to recall, more than anything else, the procession from the profane to the sacred spaces of the Athenian Acropolis. Among the historical artifacts which have most influenced Graves, the Propylaea (figure 4) holds a pre-eminent position. Like the Propylaea, the Hanselmann Residence imparts a precise spatial and temporal dimension to the activity of transition. This activity is integral to the composition, for the plane denoting the outer edge of the transition zone (the street facade) also completes the double cube.

The similarity extends to a locational correspondence between the studio house and the Temple of the Nike Aptera. Still, a larger significance for the studio house resides in the fact that it extends the opposition of solid and void into a secondary organization by establishing correspondences on the diagonal between elements which are disposed within the orthogonal grid (the studio house and the balcony and roof terrace at the southeast corner of the main house), and by establishing elements on a literally diagonal grid (the large area of ground-level paving). This distinction registers degrees of disaffiliation from the central activities of the house itself and degrees of affiliation with activities which occur within the natural order. Recreational activities are among these, and they are oriented toward the principal evidence of that natural order on the site, the stream which moves diagonally across it.

The studio house may be seen as a recapitulation in miniature of the main house, an initial offering to the visitor, and a preparation for the experience of the main house and its immediate precinct. In terms of building program, it satisfies the need to accommodate the client's avocation (weaving) by identifying it as something apart from the interdependent activities of family life. The programmatic imperative is less forceful here than it is, for example, in Le Corbusier's house for Dr. Carrutchet (figure 5) at La Plata, Argentina (another model Graves acknowledges). There, the principle of continuity in the facades along the street is acknowledged by locating the client's medical office along the sidewalk, where it serves as a middle-ground between the house and street.

The relative urbanistic and programmatic leeway which Graves enjoyed in this aspect of the problem permitted him to develop some

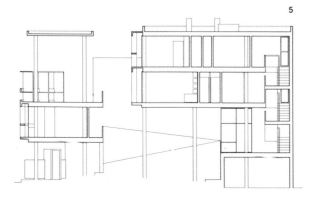

5

possibilities unavailable to Le Corbusier at La Plata. He combined the Propylaean example of ascent and penetration as the requisites of transition with that essentially Palladian conception of the piano nobile as plane of disengagement from, and observation of, the natural world. The pipe-rail extension of the studio-house frame attempts to present the street facade as idea, as organizational principle, and, therefore, as verging on the immaterial. La Plata presents the street facade first as inescapable urbanistic fact, and it is invested with an appropriate materiality and utility. In looking to both the Propylaea and La Plata for precedents, Graves repeatedly chooses the greater conceptual simplicity of the Propylaea: ascent precedes penetration at Hanselmann, and penetration is simultaneous with entry onto that idealized reference plane, the piano nobile. This plane serves functionally as more than an eyrie from which nature may be surveyed: it accommodates the collective spaces of the building and serves as a datum from which a layering of more private spaces is effected in the vertical dimension.

In the Hanselmann Residence, the geometric and constructional frameworks, in general, coincide. Graves determines the order of that unified framework by establishing a sequence of archetypal spatial experiences through his vertical and horizontal layering of the space of the composition. The Hanselmann design does not involve specifically referential, metaphoric statements in any major way. The analogy between the studio house and the Temple of the Nike Aptera seems intended primarily to bring to consciousness the universality of the spatial experience in question. Even the 'industrial' imagery which occurs here (pipe railings, etc.) has been so thoroughly assimilated into an international post-Corbusian aesthetic as to have lost most of the associational qualities which it possessed when its use was novel.

The mural in the main house, on the other hand, recapitulates aspects of the entire composition and of its geographic and cultural milieu. Unlike the studio house, the mural recapitulates illusionistically. It is a metaphoric object within a framework at once non-metaphoric and determined by an ordering of archetypal spatial experiences.

In the Benacerraf Residence Addition, which was designed after the Hanselmann Residence, a significant shift has occurred in the architect's attitude toward the relationships possible both between metaphoric and archetypal statements and between object and framework. The shift takes the form of an advocacy of selective synthesis between architecture, sculpture, and painting — or rather a selective suppression of the distinctions between these media.

What seems to have been the premise for these innovations was an increased consciousness of the correspondences which exist between man-made and natural orders. The theme of architecture as 'reasoned' artifice amid 'unreasoned' nature reappears. The opposition of the orders is again analogous to that observed at Delphi.

In the Hanselmann Residence, the composition includes an open and a closed cube in juxtaposition. At Benacerraf, the opened and closed volumes are combined into one by the provision or omission of facades. The use of color on the open, east facade is puzzling, and the ascription of metaphorical intentions in this instance cannot be made with assurance. The south facade, on the other hand, presents a convergence of object and framework, meaning and form. The pre-eminent feature of that facade is the undulating soffit of the opening in the wall of the second level. This south wall responds to nature in the literal sense by providing a partial sunbreak for the roof garden behind it.

Once again the color, texture, and continuous aspect of planar surfaces are emblematic, as they are at Hanselmann, of an aspiration toward the purity of abstraction. Structure is disposed on a system of Cartesian coordinates. Architecture-in-nature as an opposition of orders does not deny architecture as correction and completion of nature. Graves' design achieves 'completion' and 'correction' by metaphorical means. He introduces selective modification of the opposition between the natural and the man-made orders, and this modification produces some resonant ambiguities.

A high hedge bounds the property parallel to the south facade of the addition. The bottom flange of the exposed beam which carries the load of the second storey along that south facade is equivalent in height to the top of that hedge. The beam is painted green and implies dislocation between it and the rest of that green 'wall.' A fundamental distinction is blurred, and the possibility even of synthesis between a natural and a man-made phenomenon is introduced. What results is a fragmentary *allée*. An analogous image of complementarity in dislocation, this time solely between elements of the natural order, is evident in the David Hockney painting (figure 6) shown here.

The upper edge of the opening in the sun-
continued on pg. 55

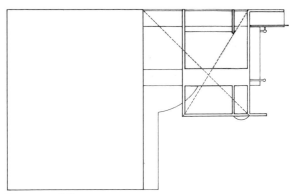

Benacerraf House

6

7

41

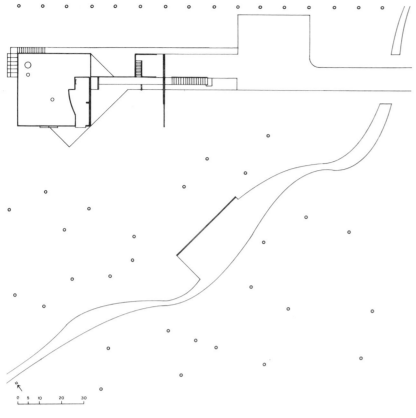

Site Plan

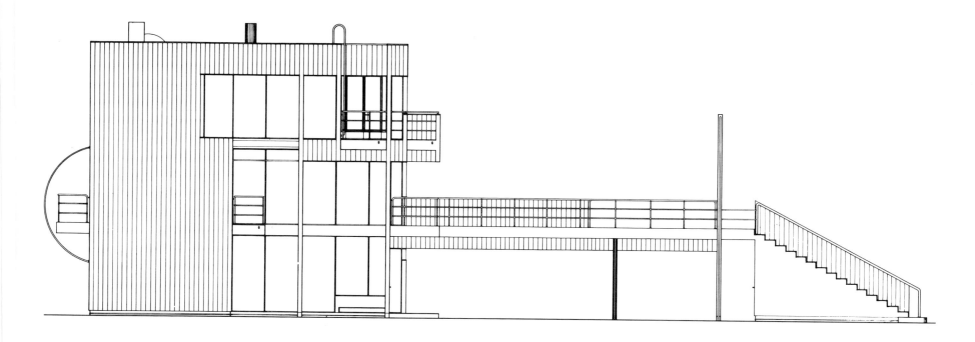

South Elevation

0 — 5

Plan Level 1

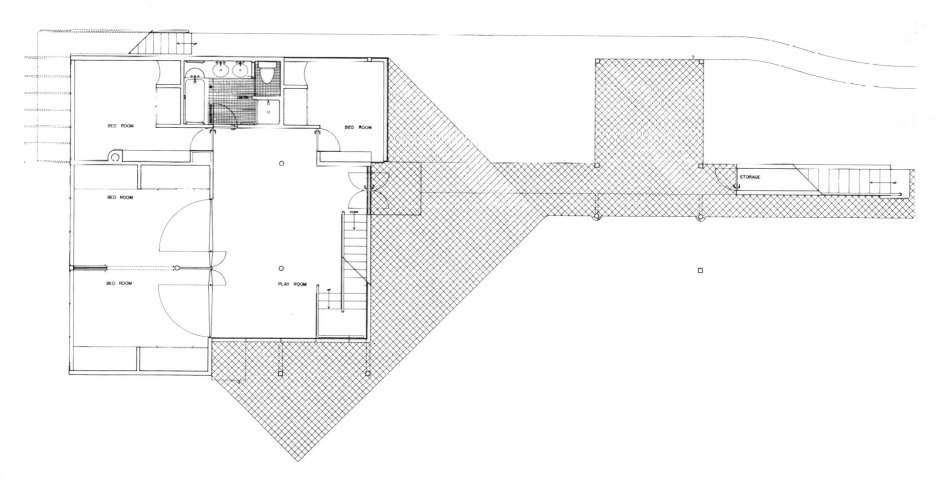

BED ROOM

BED ROOM

BED ROOM

BED ROOM

PLAY ROOM

STORAGE

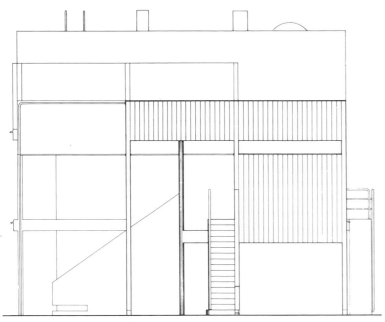

East Elevation: Studio

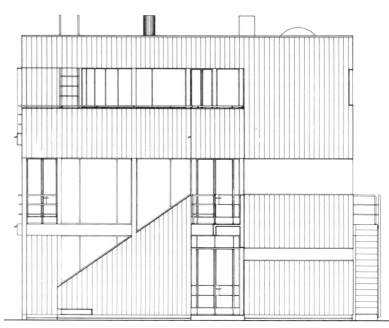

East Elevation: House

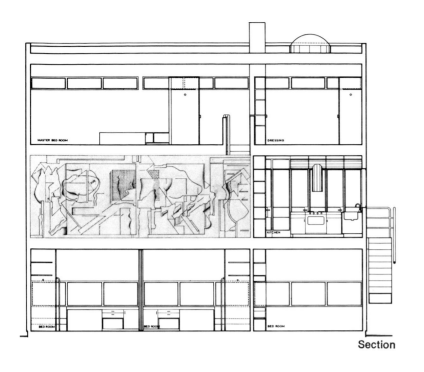

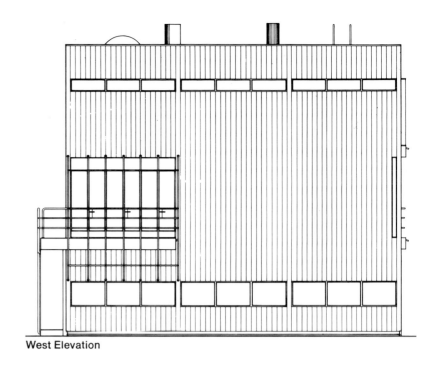

Section

West Elevation

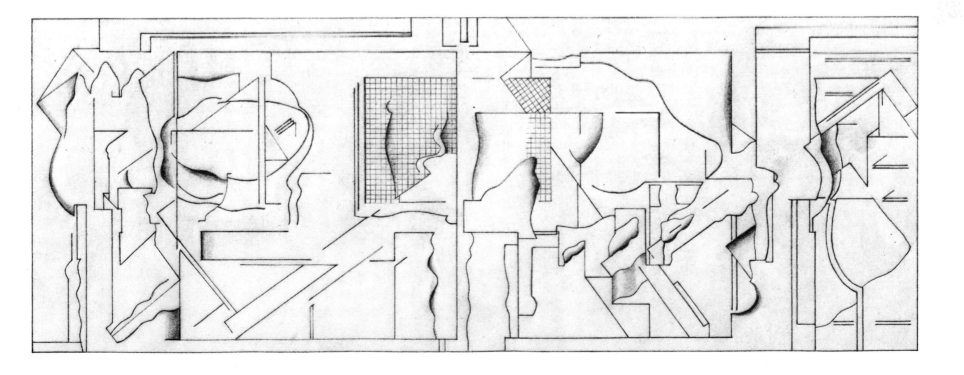

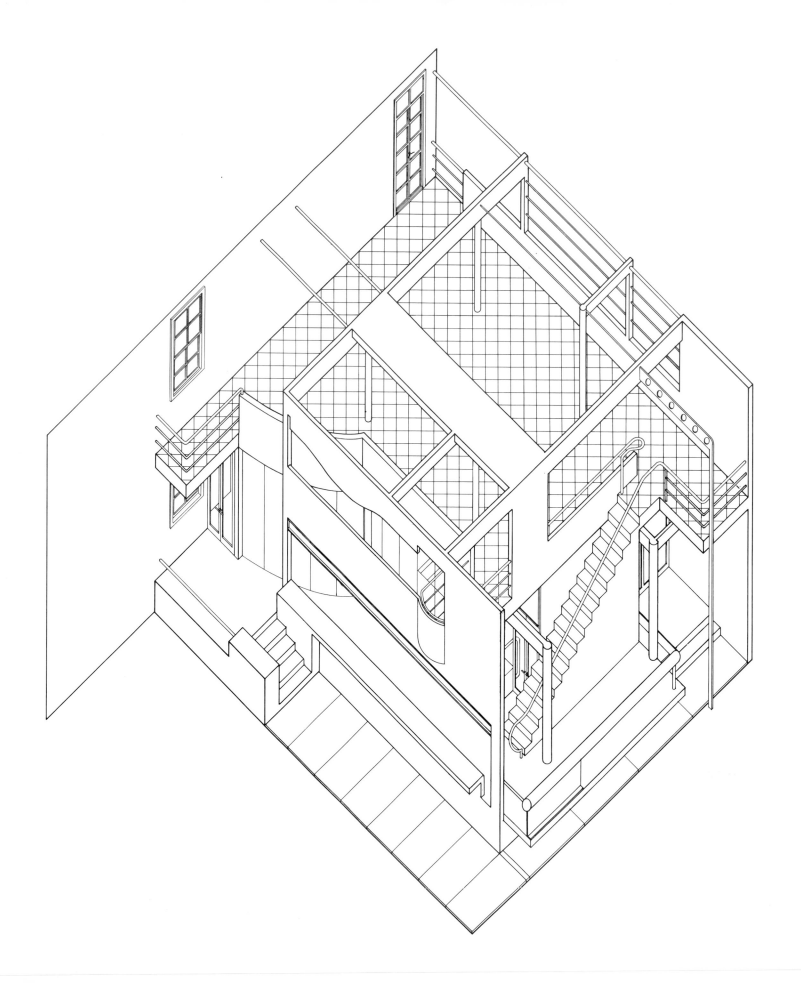

# Michael Graves

## Benacerraf House Addition 1969

continued from pg. 41

screen wall, moreover, undulates only where there is no tree beside it: it completes nature by correcting nature's omission, by creating the implication of a continuous treeline where nature did not complete the process of providing one. The artificial sunscreen compensates for the absence of the natural sunscreen. And yet the shape of the curve itself evokes much more than the outline of a row of trees that is not there. It is the s-curve so widely used by the Cubists to create a shared contour between two interlocking objects. So often it was the edge of a guitar which lent the shape which provided the Cubists with their inanimate odalisque. But, if the green beam and the hedge bounding the property may be thought to be in a sense complementary, the two elements which share the contour of the curved soffit are as fundamentally complementary as in the balustrade of Borromini's cortile at San Carlino (figure 7): we are dealing here with the inevitable complementarity of form and space.

Just as the Hanselmann Residence in its layering of spaces corresponds loosely to the stages of the initiation into a place of particularized ritual from the space of generalized activity (the experience of the Acropolis), the Benacerraf Residence Addition re-presents in architectural form aspects of the natural cosmos as the architect idealizes them. The roof terrace re-establishes the ground plane as an ideal construct. This is by no means a novel phenomenon, but Graves' utilization of the theme of representation of aspects of the physical world is more extensive, and more self-conscious than that of Le Corbusier. As primitive man, according to Eliade,[8] would embody his divinely revealed vision of the cosmos in the design of his house, Graves extends his concern with re-presenting the natural world beyond that resurrected ground plane: the sky becomes the infinite ceiling of an implied room when the trees become the columns engaged by the wall of that room.

The validity of employing a metaphor in architecture is severely limited by the factor of scale. The artificial treeline at Benacerraf has a meaning that is determined partly by its size in relation to what it represents. This observation is, in a sense, a corollary to Le Corbusier's contention regarding scale of design and degree of geometric abstraction. The

architectural suggestion of a treeline at the scale of a city or of a sector of a city, would be absurd. However, as Graves acknowledges in the Hanselmann Residence, metaphoric and archetypal formal statements can be of an equally complex resonance in their response to the exigencies of the natural order.

A building by Mies continues to be valid urbanistically precisely because it is ignorant of anything but itself: that its surroundings (and even its use) may change is pre-supposed by the architect, and the consistency of the building's logic is therefore not dependent on physical context. The formal responsiveness of the Hanselmann Residence and the Benacerraf Residence Addition to their actual and their idealized contexts is, in contrast, an enduring index of the symbolic import of those contexts. Each of these artifacts is, in one sense, the history of a particular place at a particular time. And yet, if that context were to change, the validity of the artifact would be enhanced rather than diminished, for it would have become the memory of the city.

Le Corbusier defined the city as man's occupation of the plain. Geometry is the system of that occupation; architecture is the manifestation of that system in space. The public framework of the street modulates the collective privacies of that interior city, the piano nobile. And the city's roofs may become the ground again—rectified, idealized. In this city the principle of mutual responsiveness takes on a luminous potential. Each new building acknowledges not only its own uses and the presence of its surroundings but some vision of the significance of the components of those surroundings, and, ultimately, some vision of the world. A network of ever-increasing correspondences results, and with each change in that network, the meaning of the city becomes more vast and more profound.

Photo Credits:
Fig. 1. Architectural Design.
Fig. 2. Collection of Paul Benacerraf.
Fig. 3. Photograph by the author.
Fig. 4. Photograph by Michael Graves.
Fig. 5. Drawing by Ruth Goodman.
Fig. 6. Studio International.
Fig. 7. Paolo Portoghesi, The Rome of Borromini.
Figures 1-7 either photographed or re-photographed by Laurin McCracken.

1. Le Corbusier: The City of Tomorrow, M.I.T. Press, Cambridge, 1971; p. 40.
2. Aldo Van Eyck: in Team 10 Primer, M.I.T. Press, Cambridge, 1968; pp. 41-44.
3. Herbert Read: The Philosophy of Modern Art, World Publishing Co., Cleveland, 1954; p. 75.
4. Ibid, p. 75.
5. Ibid, p. 75.
6. Daniel-Henry Kahnweiler: Juan Gris, His Life and Work, Harry N. Abrams, Inc., New York (copyright in France, 1946, by Gallimard), revised edition; p. 218.
7. Le Corbusier: The Modulor, M.I.T. Press, Cambridge, 1968; p. 218.
8. Mircea Eliade's provocative discussion of sacred and profane space, which has informed much of the thinking in this article, may be found in Chapter One of his book, The Sacred and the Profane, Harcourt, Brace and World, Inc., New York, 1959; pp. 20-65.

William La Riche
Lecturer, Architecture and Visual Arts,
Princeton University

Site Plan

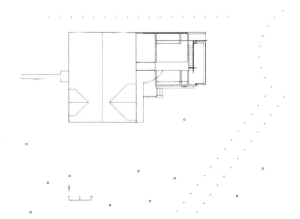

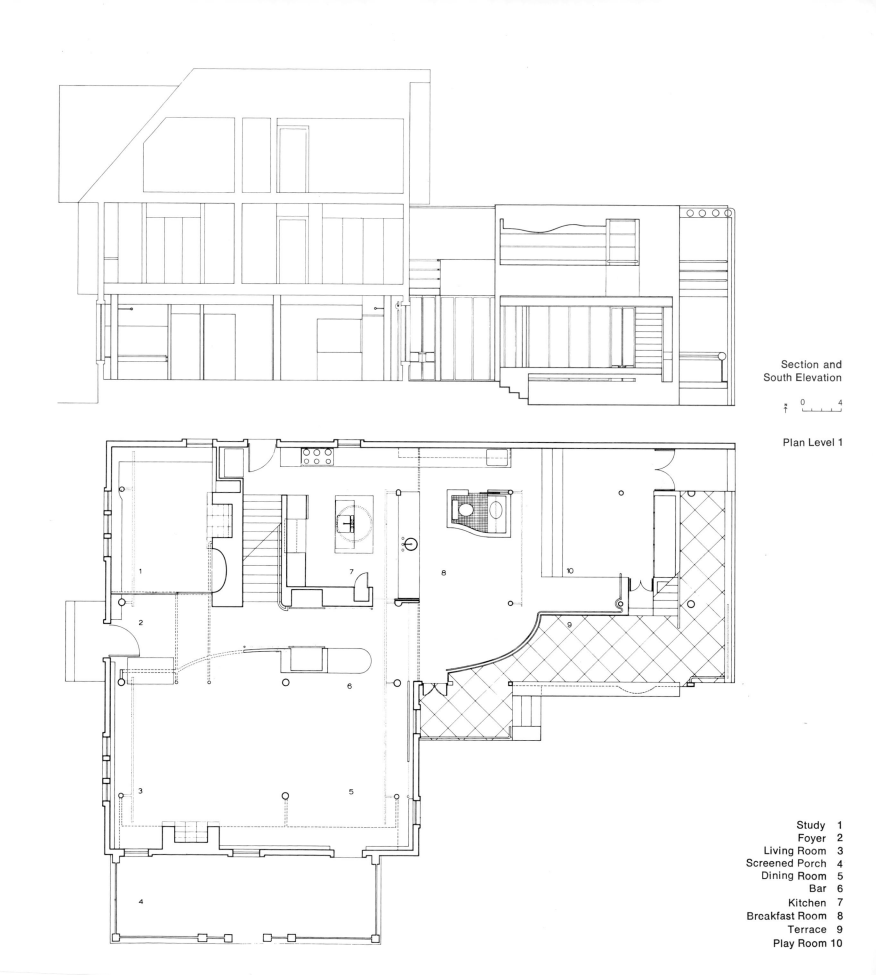

Section and
South Elevation

↑ N  0 |——| 4

Plan Level 1

Study 1
Foyer 2
Living Room 3
Screened Porch 4
Dining Room 5
Bar 6
Kitchen 7
Breakfast Room 8
Terrace 9
Play Room 10

Section

0 ⌐—┴—┴—┘ 4  N↑

Plan Level 2

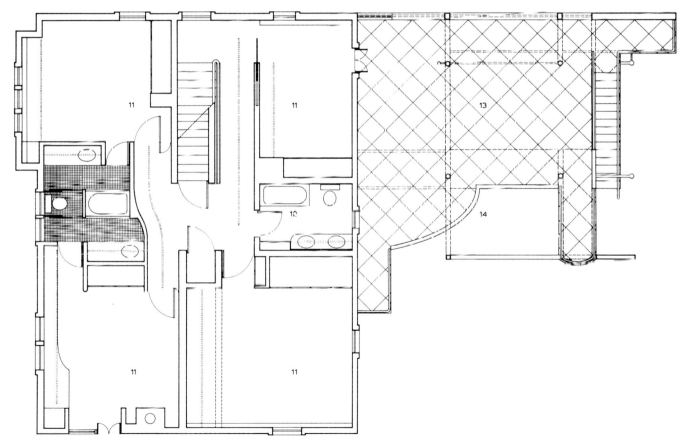

11 Bedroom
12 Bathroom
13 Terrace
14 Void

# Charles Gwathmey

## Gwathmey Residence and Studio   1966

**Site**

One acre field with ocean view on southern shore of Long Island.

**Program**

Residence and studio for painter and textile designer.

**Construction**

Slab on grade, wood frame, cedar siding (exterior and interior).

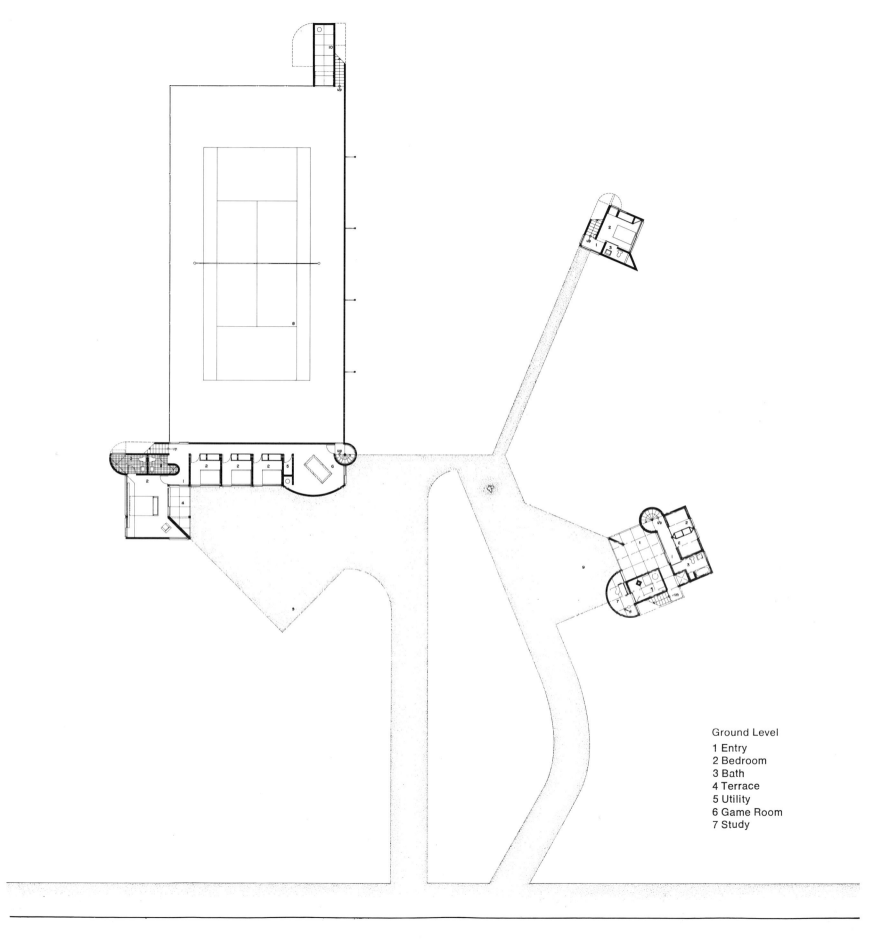

Ground Level
1 Entry
2 Bedroom
3 Bath
4 Terrace
5 Utility
6 Game Room
7 Study

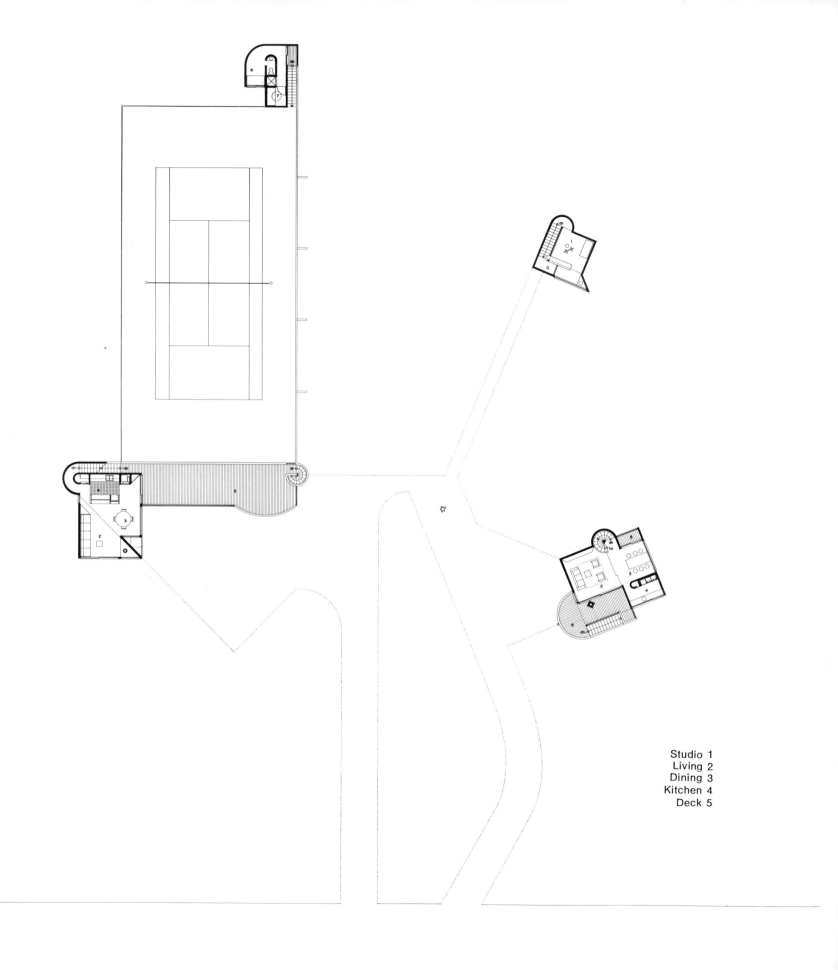

Studio 1
Living 2
Dining 3
Kitchen 4
Deck 5

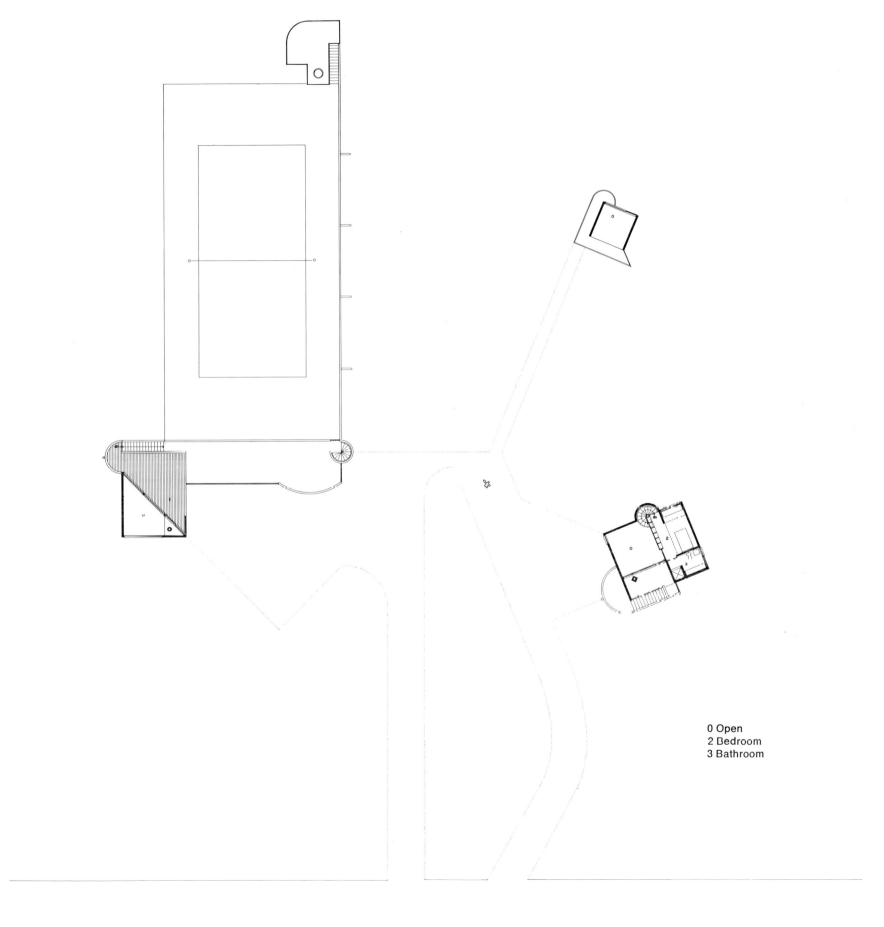

0 Open
2 Bedroom
3 Bathroom

69

# Charles Gwathmey

## Bridgehampton Residences   1970

### Site
Two acre ocean dune on southern shore of Long Island.

### Program
Two residences designed and built concurrently for same family (father/son) with totally different programs.

### Construction
Slab on grade, wood frame, cedar siding (exterior and interior).

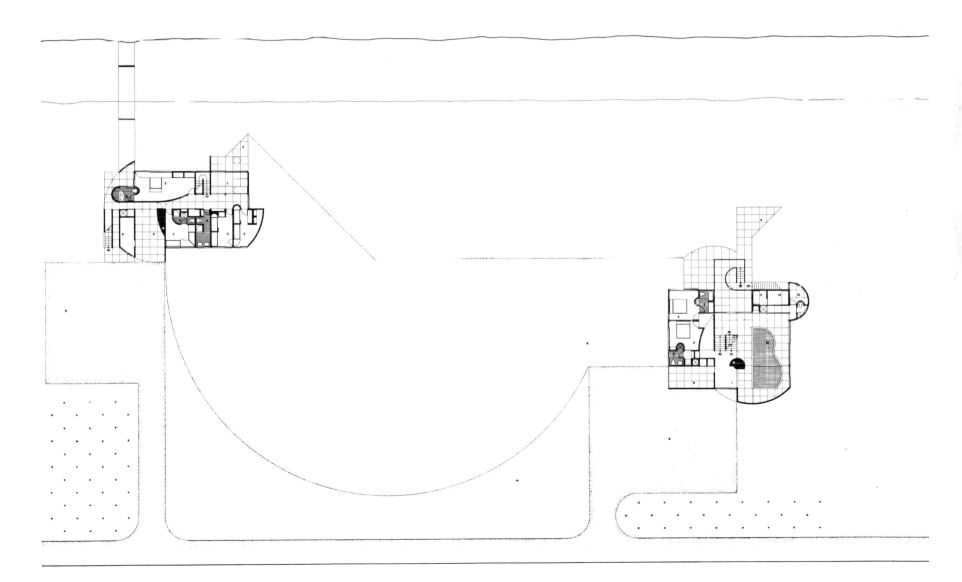

Site Plan

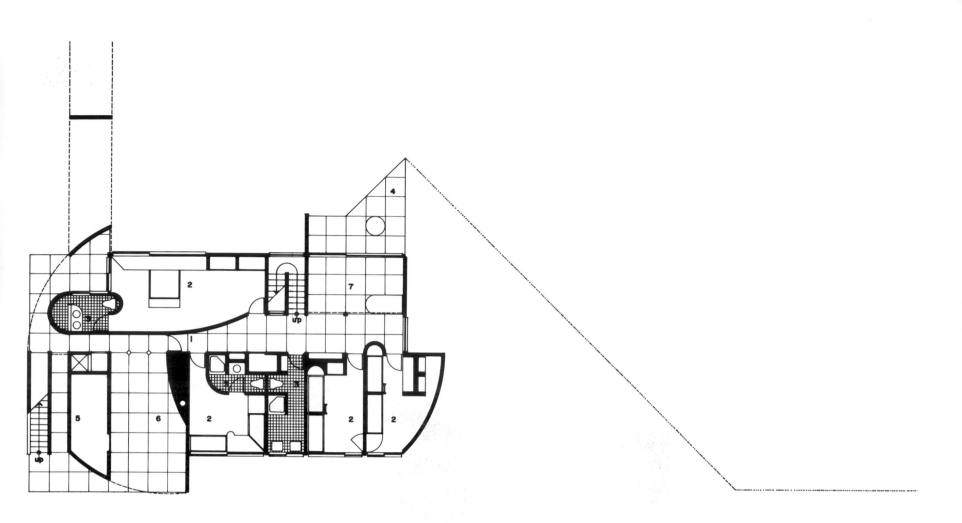

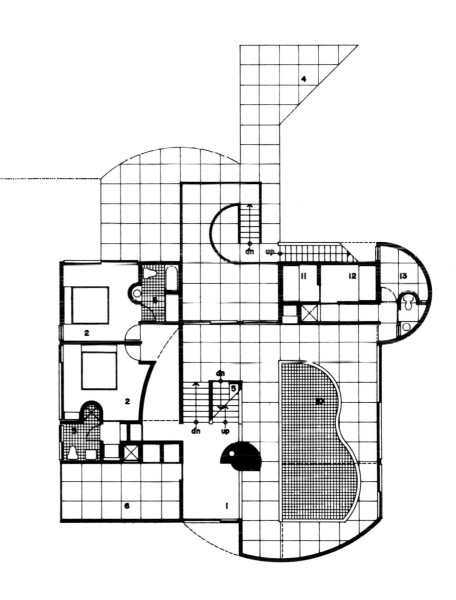

Ground Level
 1 Entry
 2 Bedroom
 3 Bath
 4 Terrace
 5 Utility
 6 Garage
 7 Play Room
 8 Lawn
 9 Parking
10 Pool
11 Steam Room
12 Sauna
13 Dressing

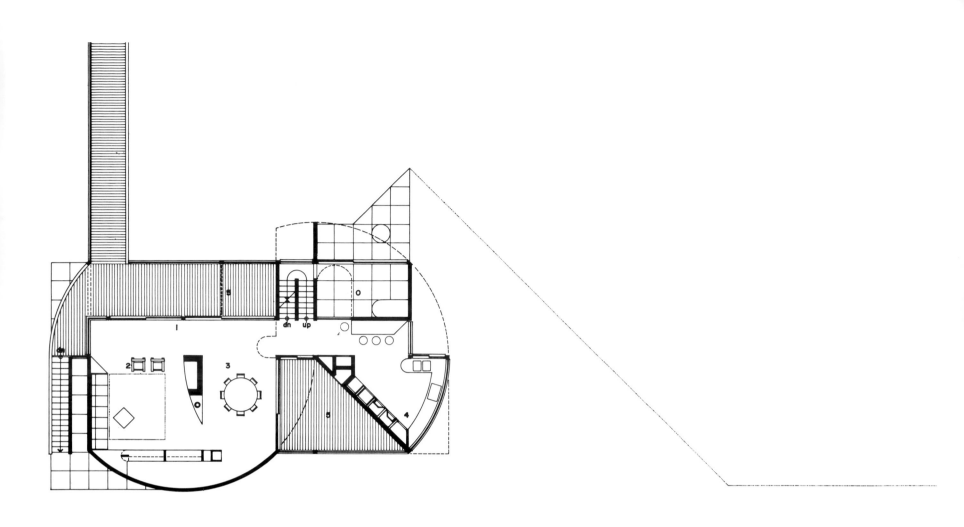

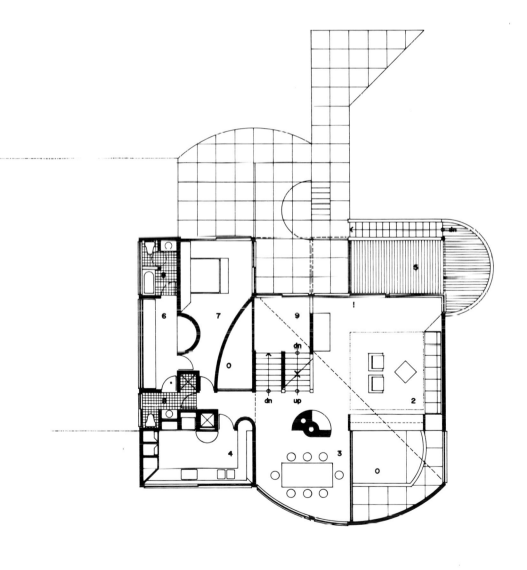

Living Level
1 Entry
2 Living
3 Dining
4 Kitchen
5 Deck
6 Dressing
7 Bedroom
8 Bath
9 Landing

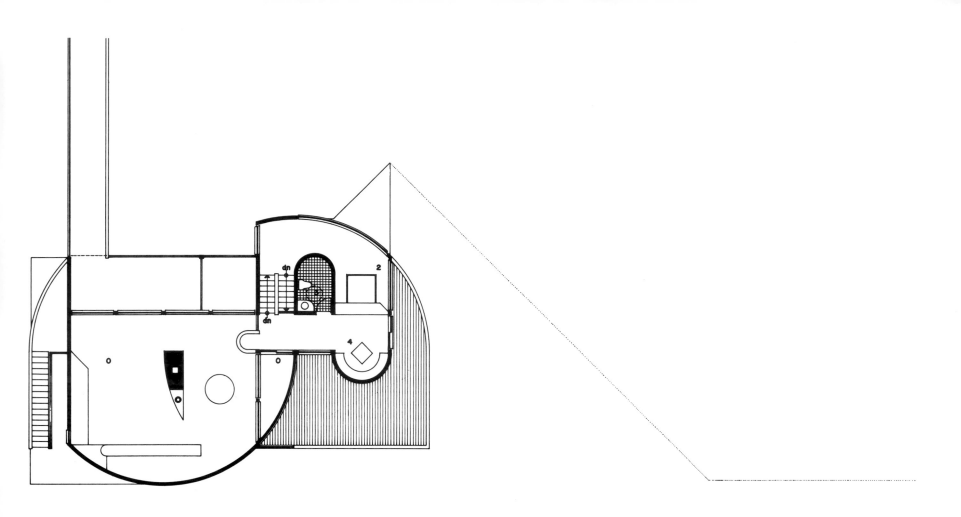

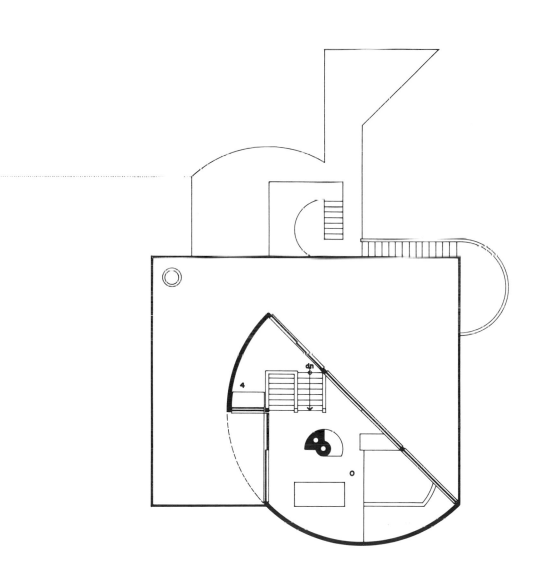

Upper Level
1 Deck
2 Bedroom
3 Bath
4 Study

Longitudinal Section

Cross Section

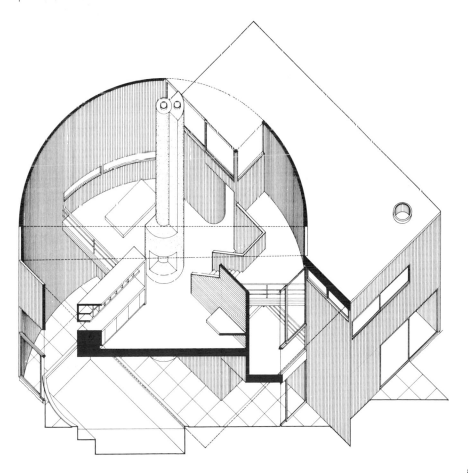

# John Hejduk

## House 10   1966

**Program**

Garage
Walk
Entry
Living
Dining
Kitchen
Gallery
Storage
Bathroom
Bedroom

**Surfaces**

Glass As Shown
Interior Walls—White
Exterior Walls—Stainless Steel or Chrome

**Idea-Concept**

Horizontal Extension
Hypotenuse
Three-Quarter Figure
Point-Line-Plane-Volume
Bio-Morphic—Bio-Technic
Structure
Time
Projection

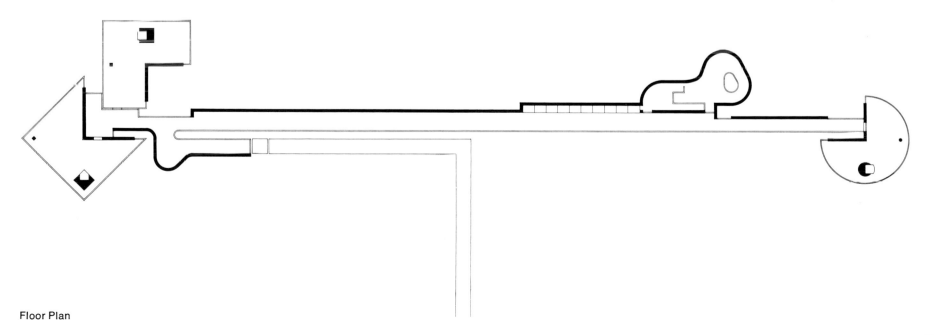

Floor Plan

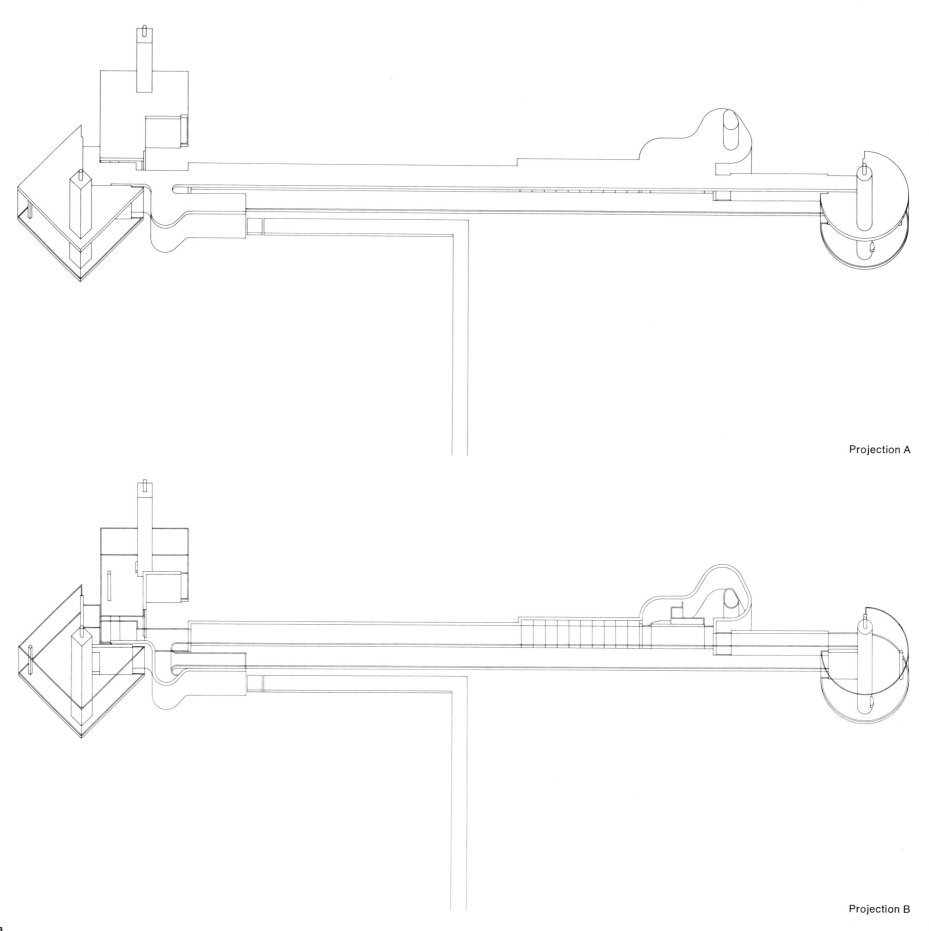

Projection A

Projection B

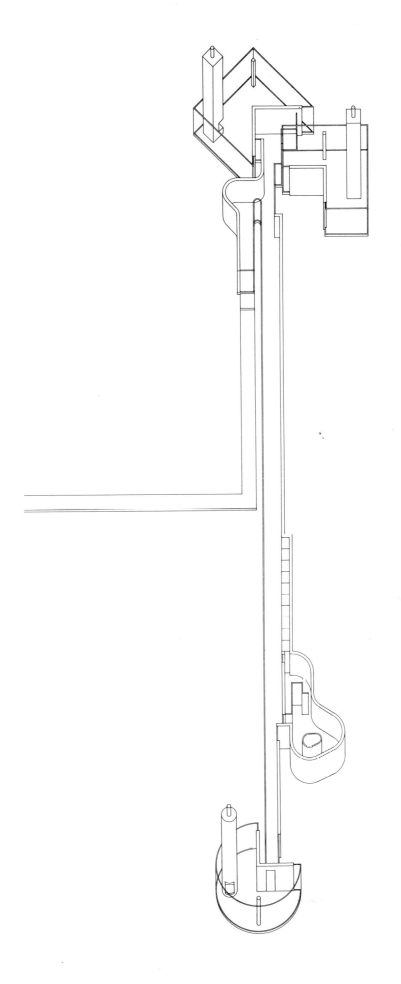

Projection C

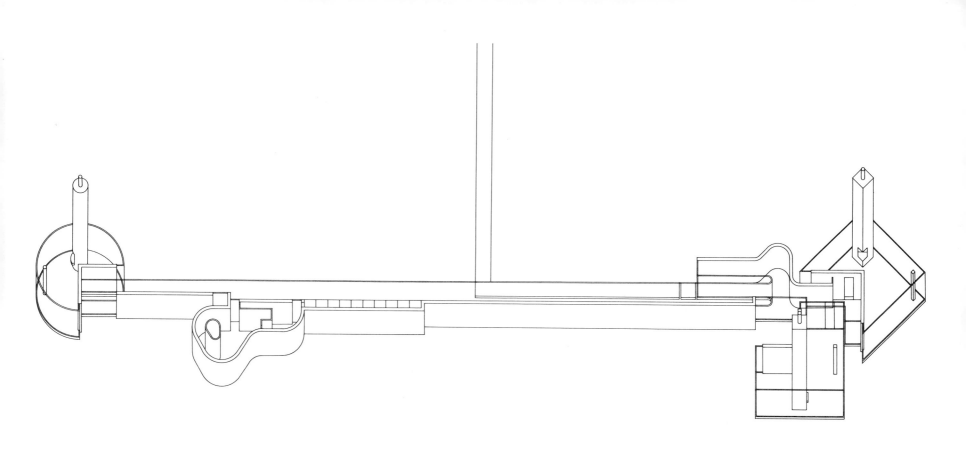

Projection D

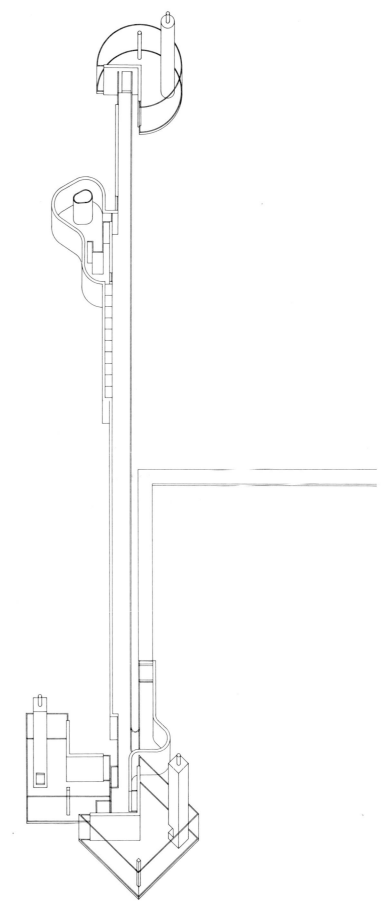

Projection E

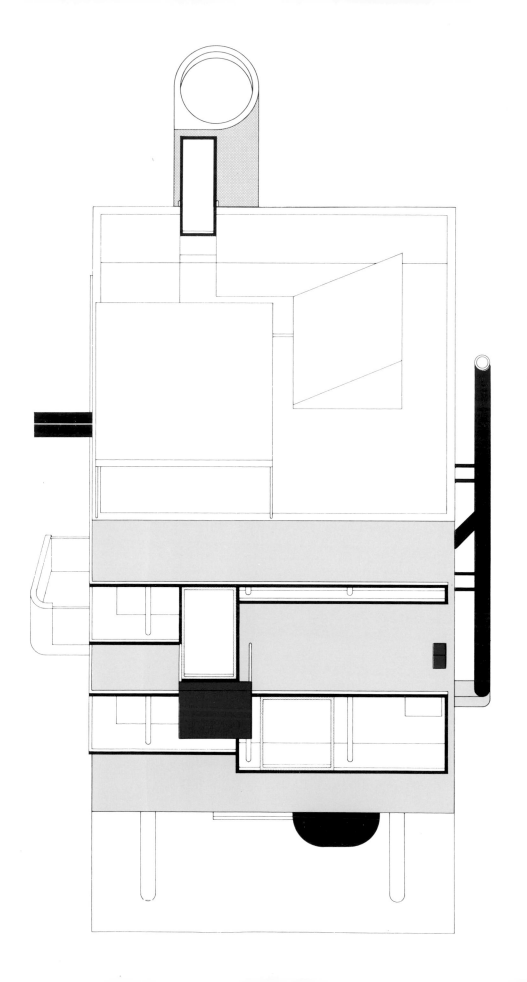

Color Projection

# John Hejduk

Bernstein House  1968

**Program**
House

**Surfaces**
Exterior—yellow, blue, red, black, white, gray

**Idea-Concept**
Color—exterior-primaries, interior-white

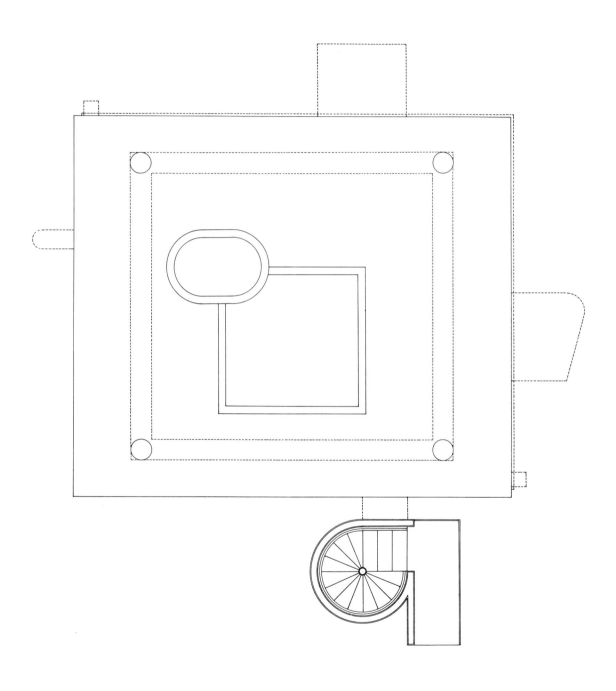

First Floor Plan

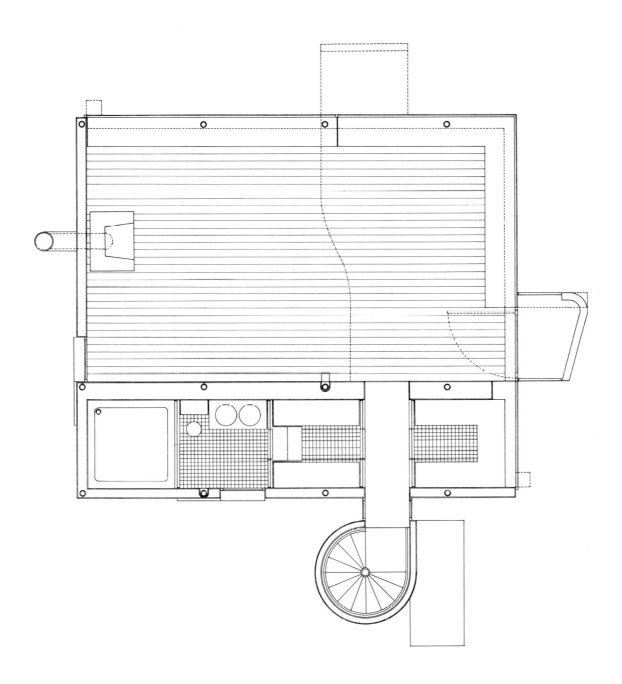

Second Floor Plan

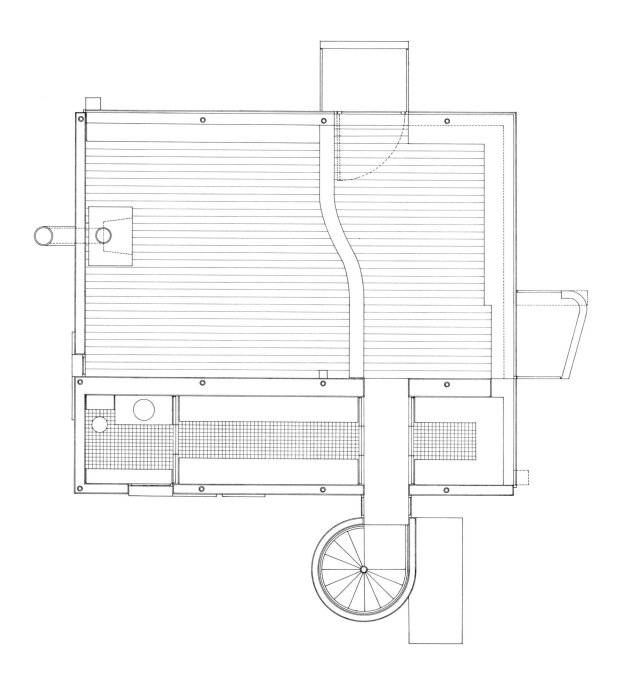

Third Floor Plan

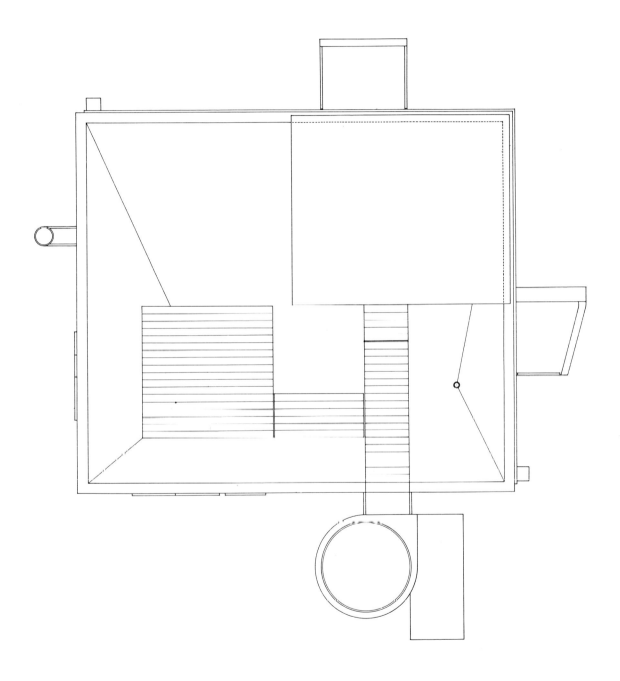

Roof Plan

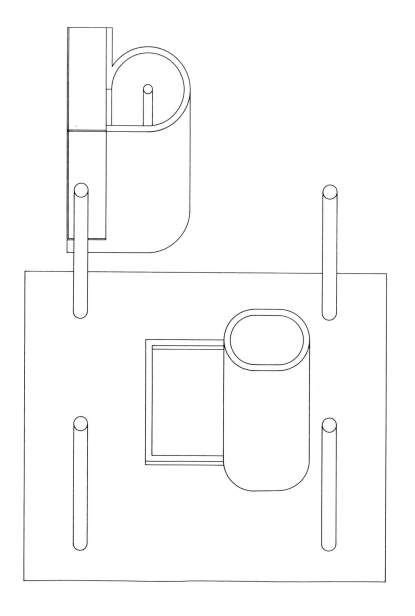

Projection A

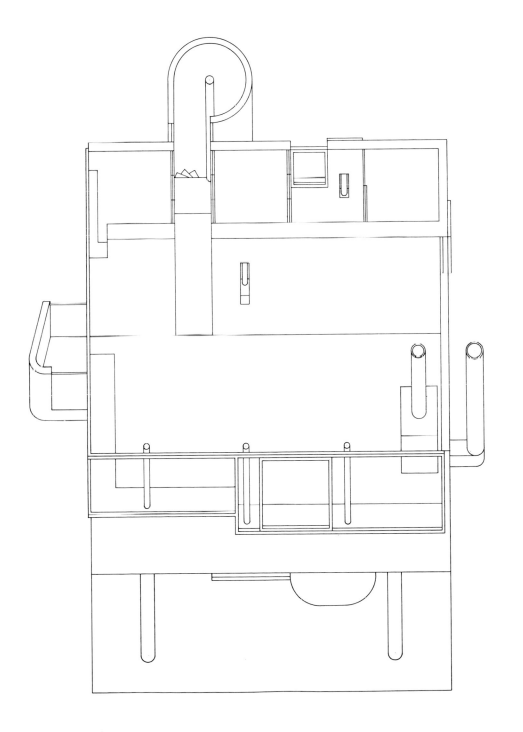

Projection B

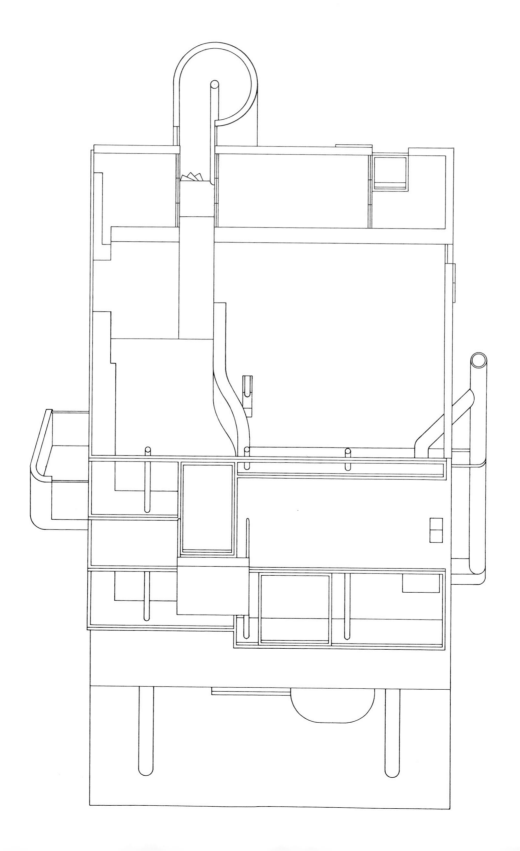

Projection C

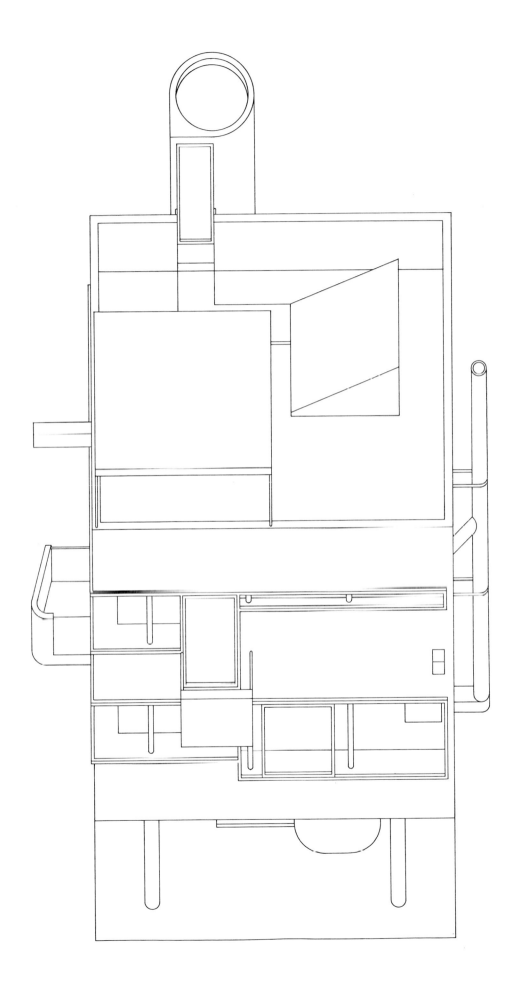

Projection D

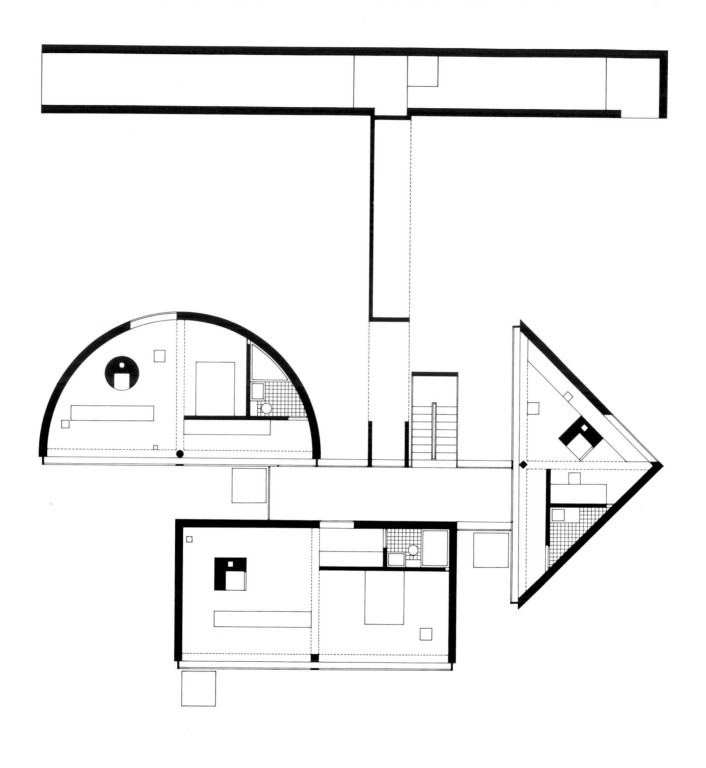

First Floor Plan

# John Hejduk

## One-Half House   1966

**Program**

Entry walk
Living
Dining
Kitchen
Music-Library
Bathrooms
Bedrooms

**Surfaces**

Glass as shown
Interior walls—white
Exterior walls—white

**Idea-Concept**

One half of a square
One half of a circle
One half of a diamond

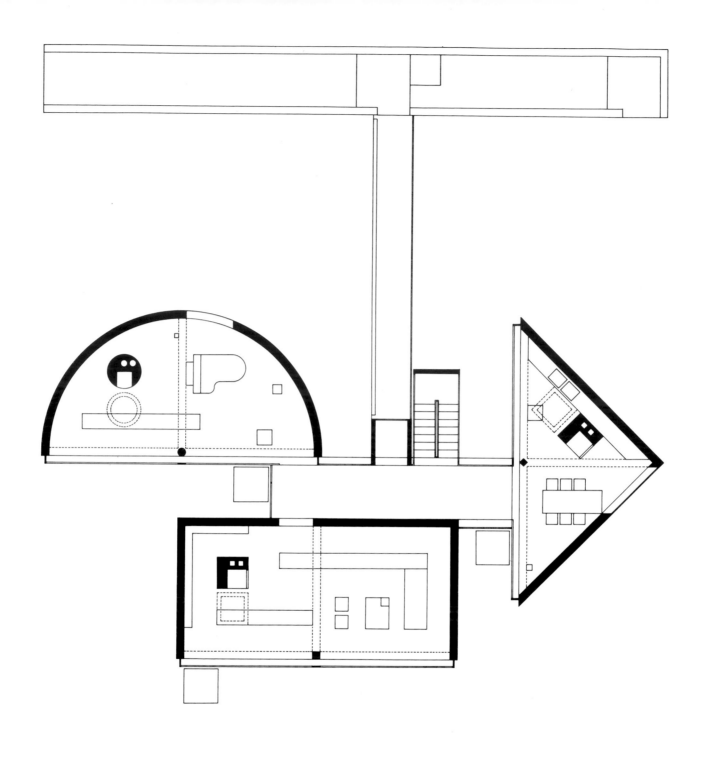

Second Floor Plan

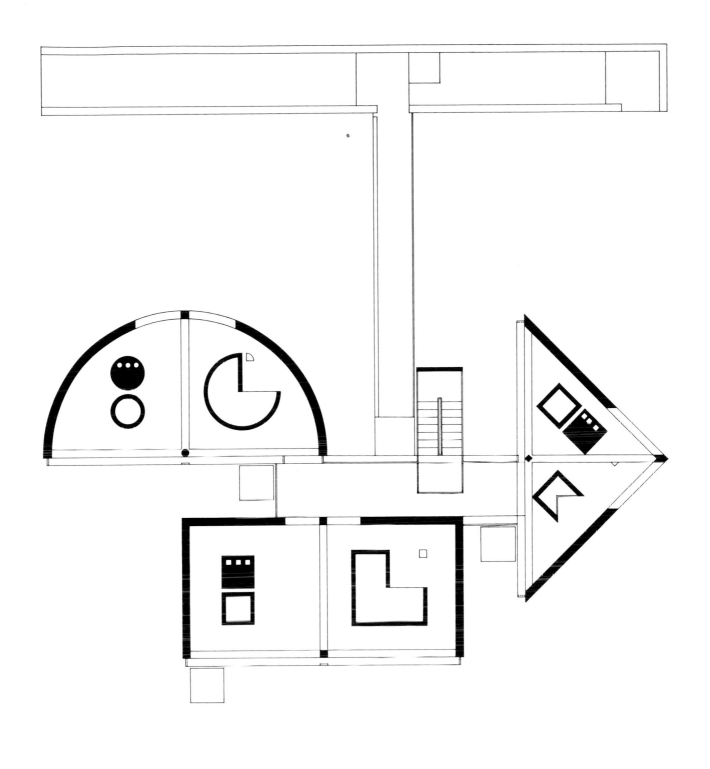

Roof Plan

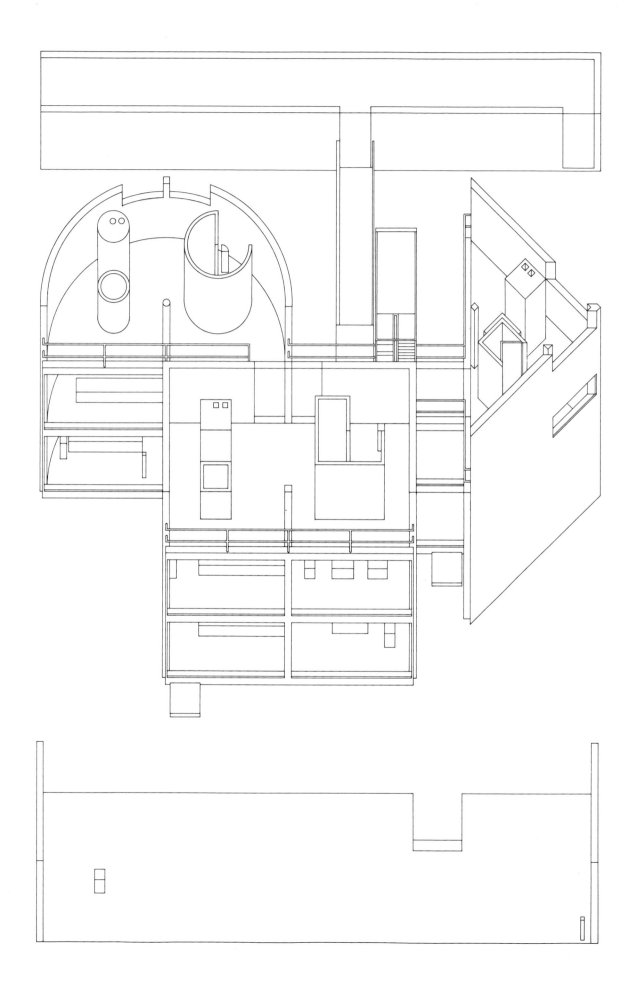

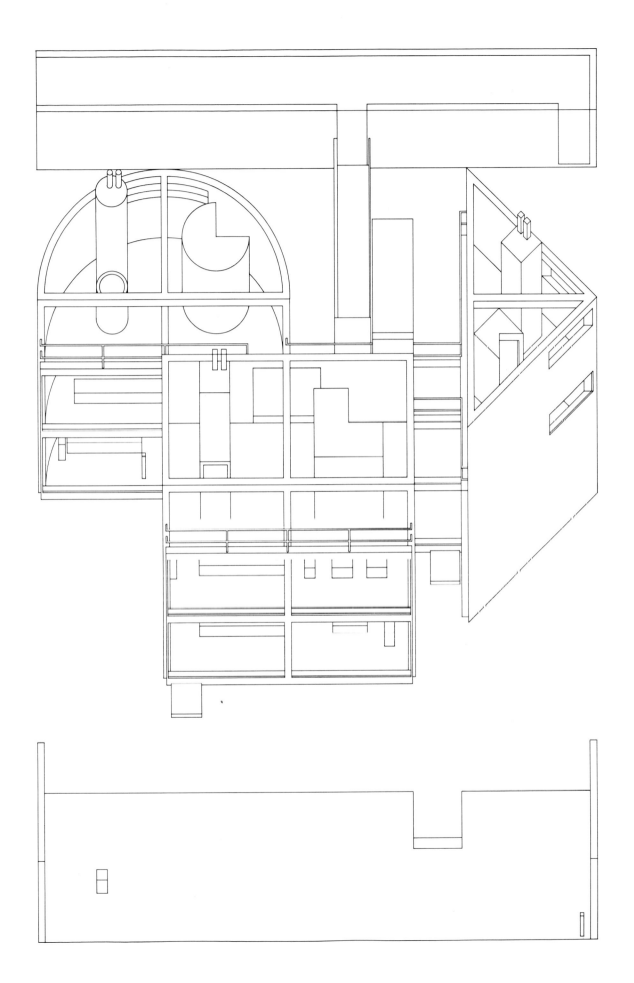

Projection D

# Richard Meier

## Smith House    1965

"Mankind is now in one of its rare moods of shifting its outlook." It is the business of architects, as with Whitehead's philosophers and businessmen, "to re-create and re-enact a vision of the world, including those elements of reverence and order without which society lapses into a riot, and penetrated through and through with unflinching rationality."

There are two aspects to the concept of the house; one ideal and abstract, the other real and analytical. These aspects are interdependent.

The abstract concept of the Smith House is the idea of a spatially layered linear system with circulation across and along the layers. Corollary to this is the acceptance of the problem, inherent in any linear system, of ending that system.

The ideal aspect of the concept, the 'vision of the world,' affects and is affected by its real and analytical response to problems related to site, program, circulation and entrance, structure and enclosure.

### Site

The Smith House is set among rocks and trees on a 1½ acre site that overlooks Long Island Sound. There are dense evergreens at the entrance; the land clears and rises to the center of the site, then drops sharply to the rocky shoreline and falls away on one side to a sand beach. These natural changes in character and elevation have dominant direction and may be seen, like geological strata, as layers. The sense of progression in moving across the site from entrance road to sea is reinforced by crossing the layers and this direction creates the site axis.

The building, placed near the top of the slope that descends to the water, is readily seen as spatially sequential, i.e. layered in an orthogonal progression with reference to the site axis. Approach and entrance as well as access and views to the water are across the layers, and the solid front plane must be penetrated in order to enter the layering sequence. This experience is completed and reversed by the transparent back plane of the building, and the position of the solid fireplace in this plane opposite the entrance is a barrier, semi-metaphorical, to the short circuiting of the sequence.

### Program

The house is for a family with two children, and the organization of the plan is expressive of the programmatic separation of the public and private areas of family life. Reference to the spatial sequence in terms of layers or zones extends that vertical stratification of space generated by the organization of the plan. This stratification is parallel with and emphasized by the physical plane of entry. It is literal in reference to 'closed' and 'open,' but should be understood as a spatial metaphor because the literal layers, i.e. horizontal levels, within the layers are continuous between them to accommodate programmatic and social interaction. Thus the private zone is a series of 'closed' cellular spaces on three levels, and the levels of the public zone exist as three platforms within a single volume.

### Circulation

The horizontal interior circulation connects the cells of the private zone together and also relates the private zone to the public zone. It also exists as a layer between the two zones and mediates spatially between them. The location of the vertical circulation at diagonally opposed ends, as well as the stepped section of platforms within the open volume, implies diagonal transference within the primary orthogonal organization, and acknowledges the diagonal fall and magnificent outlook to cove and beach at the side of the site.

### Entrance

Entrance is controlled first within the field implied by the front plane of the building, then directed along the line of gravel entrance path and ramp to penetrate the solid front wall, which is cut away to express a pulling through of the 'open' zone on the opposite side of the house. Conversely the shift from entrance to interior circulation is signalled by the closing of the transparent back plane opposite the entrance.

### Structure and Enclosure

The dialectic of 'open' and 'closed' is extended to the structure and its enclosure of wood and glass. The private or 'closed' zone is a wood bearing wall with openings pierced in its wood surface; while the exterior walls of the 'open' zone freed by an independent structure of columns and beams, are almost entirely a glass skin in which the columns are reflected as wood mullions. Both wood and glass are seen as a skin tautly stretched over the outside of the building in which the inherent opposition of solid and transparent is brought together in the function of enclosure.

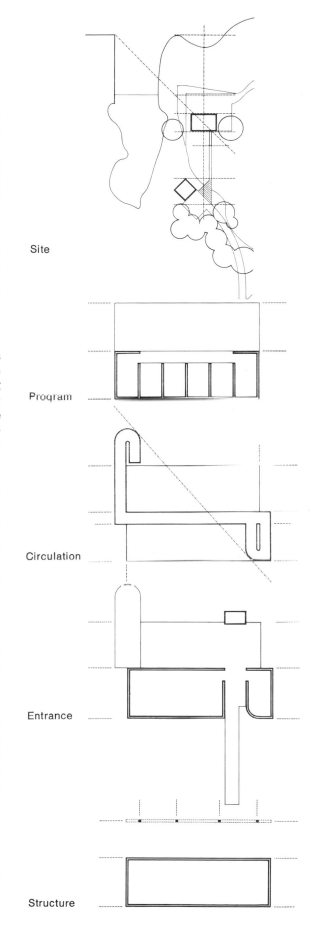

Site

Program

Circulation

Entrance

Structure

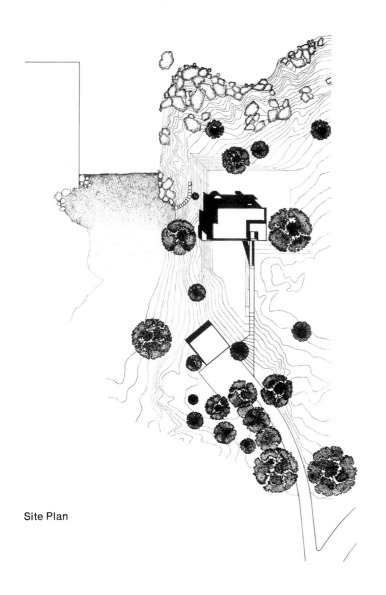

Site Plan

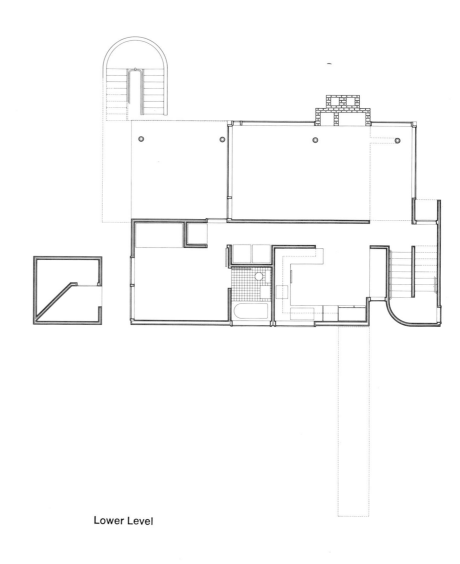

Lower Level

Section

Section

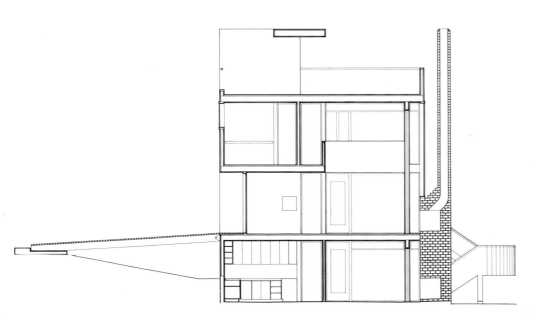

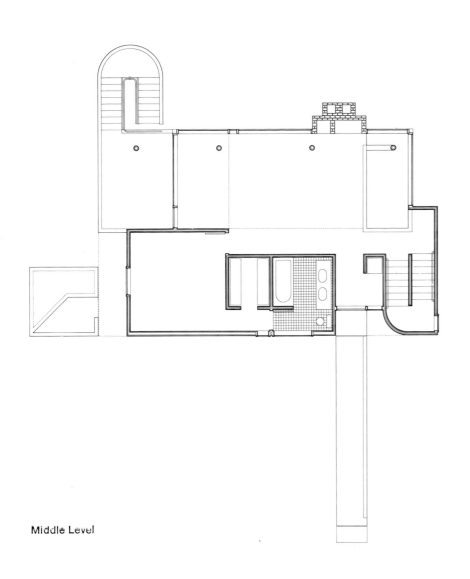

Middle Level

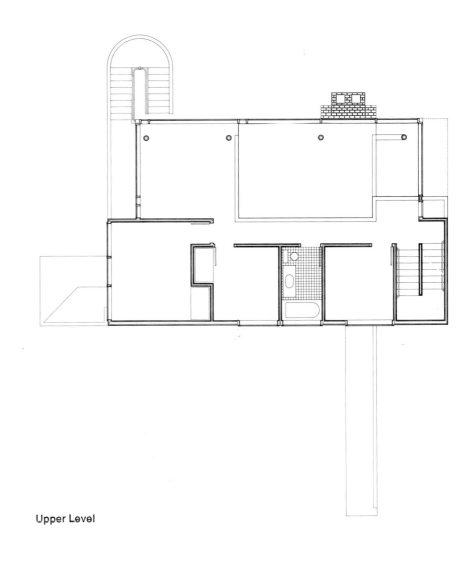

Upper Level

Northwest Elevation

Southeast Elevation

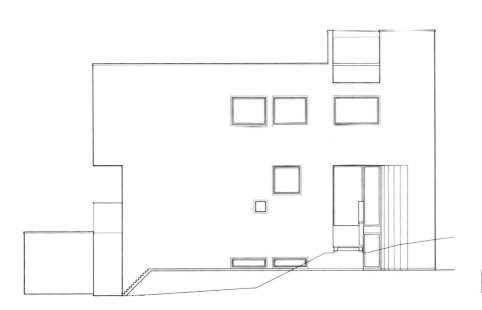

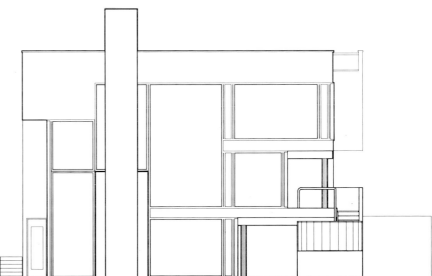

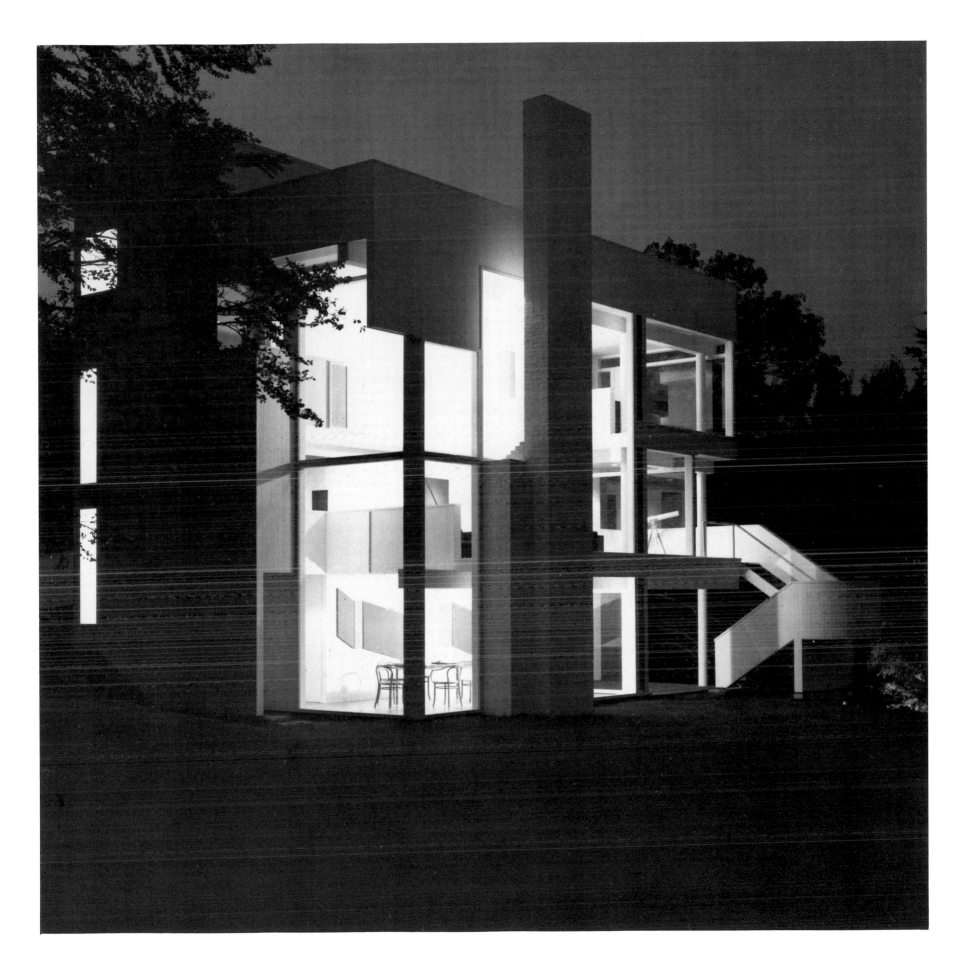

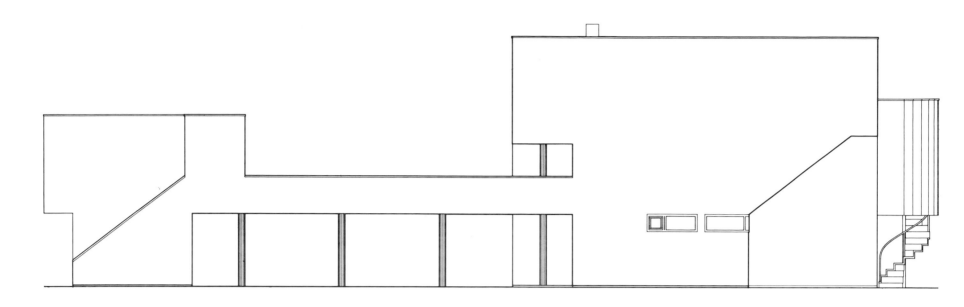

North Elevation

Lower Level

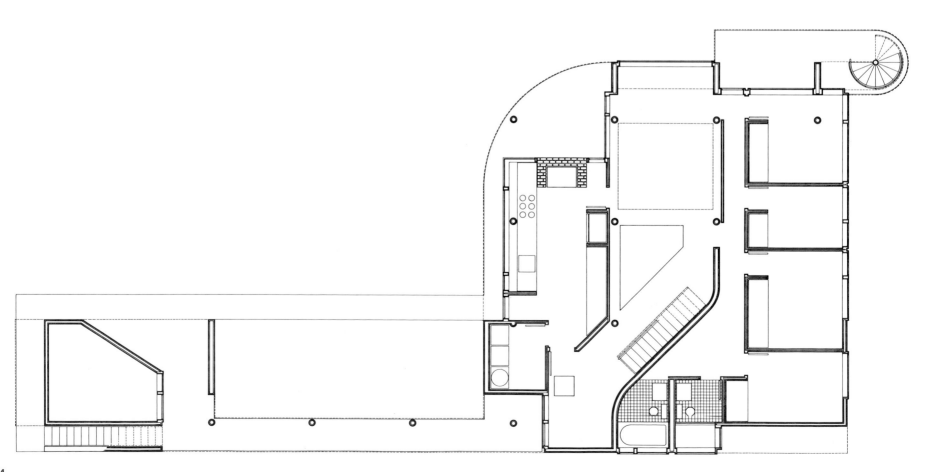

South Elevation

Middle Level

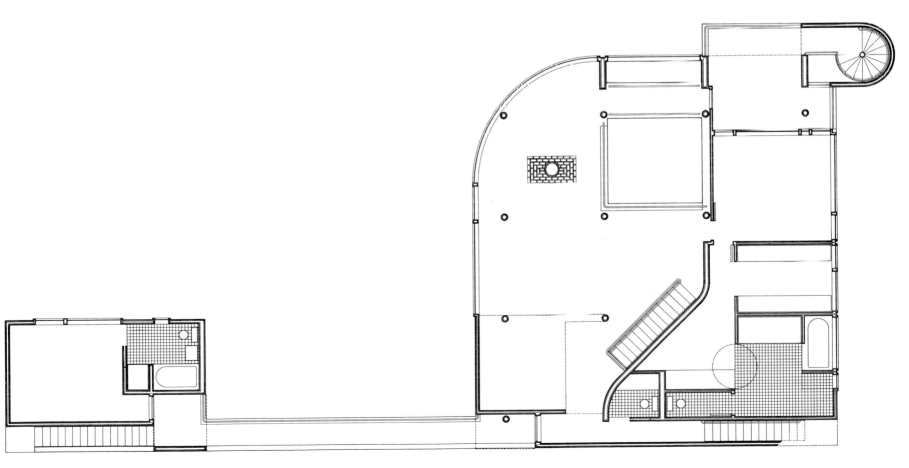

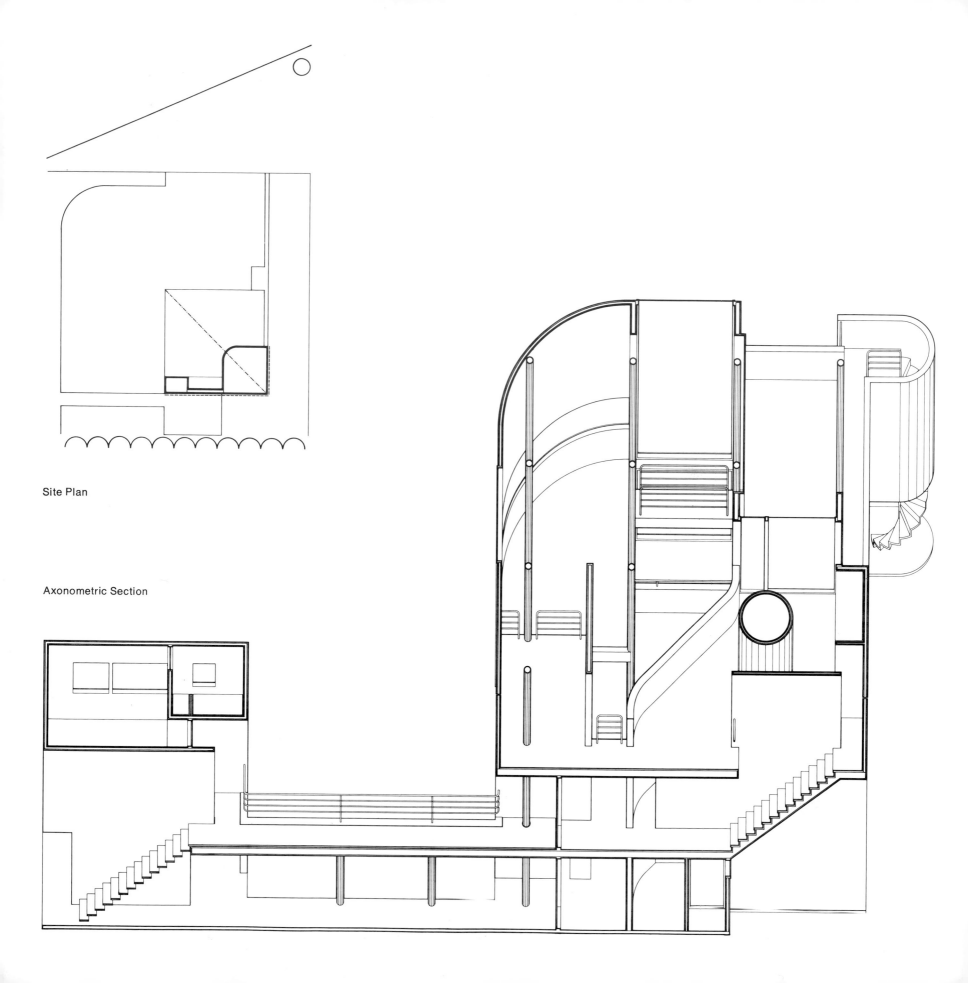

Site Plan

Axonometric Section

# Acknowledgements

### Peter Eisenman
House I: Pavilion for antique toys; Client: Mr. & Mrs. Bernard M. Barenholtz; Location: Princeton, New Jersey; Date of Construction: 1967-1968; Contractor: Bard Construction Co., Roosevelt, New Jersey; Architect: Peter Eisenman A.I.A.; Assistants: Russell Swanson, Robinson O. Brown; Drawings: Russell Swanson, Thomas Pritchard, Gregory A. Gale; Photographs: Richard Frank; Publication: Progressive Architecture, May 1968; The Architecture of Museums: catalogue of an exhibition, Museum of Modern Art, September 1968.
House II: Client: Mr. & Mrs. Richard Falk; Location: Hardwick, Vermont; Date of Construction: 1969-1970; Contractor: Dutton Smith, Middlebury, Vt.; Structural Engineer: Geiger-Berger; Architect: Peter Eisenman A.I.A.; Assistants: Gregory A. Gale, Robinson O. Brown; Drawings: Gregory A. Gale, Judith Turner, Christopher Chimera; Photographs: Norman McGrath, Gregory A. Gale; Publication: Progressive Architecture, March 1972; Architecture + Urbanism, September 1972.

### Michael Graves
Benacerraf House: Client: Prof. and Mrs. Paul Benacerraf; Location: Princeton, New Jersey; Date of Construction: 1969; Contractor: Nick Mauro; Architect: Michael Graves A.I.A.; Assistants: Robert White, Peter Waldman; Drawings: Robert White, Ruth Goodman, Bruce Abbey, Christopher Chimera; Photographs: Laurin McCracken; Publications: House and Garden, May, 1971; Progressive Architecture, March, 1972; Architecture + Urbanism, September, 1972; Arkitektur DK #2, 1972.
Hanselmann House: Client: Mr. and Mrs. Jay B. Hanselmann; Location: Ft. Wayne, Indiana; Date of Construction: 1968; Contractor: Owners; Architect: Michael Graves A.I.A.; Assistants: Timothy Wood, Peter Waldman, Peter Carl, Robert White, Christopher Chimera; Drawings: Timothy Wood, Peter Waldman; Photographs: Peter Carl, Tom Yee, House and Garden magazine; Publications: Progressive Architecture, March, 1972; Architecture + Urbanism, September, 1972; Architecture + Urbanism, November, 1972.

### Charles Gwathmey
Gwathmey Residence and Studio: Client: Mr. & Mrs. Robert Gwathmey; Location: Amagansett, New York; Date of Construction: 1966-67; Contractor: John Caramagna, John Barbagallo, Sam Castorino, Charles Gwathmey; Architect: Charles Gwathmey, Richard Henderson; Drawings: Timothy Wood; Photographs: David Hirsch, William Maris; Publications: Architectural Forum—April 1966, Architectural Forum—February 1967, House Beautiful—July 1966, New York Times Magazine—April 10, 1966, Art in America—June 1971, Interiors—July 1972; Architectural League of New York, 40 Under 40 Show 1966.
Bridgehampton Residences; Location: Bridgehampton, New York; Date of Construction: 1970; Contractor: John Caramagna, Charles Gwathmey; Architect: Charles Gwathmey; Drawings: Timothy Wood; Photographs: William Maris; Publications: House & Garden—March 1971, AIA Honor Award—1971, Art in America—January 1971.

### John Hejduk
House 10: Assistant: Richard Cordts.
Bernstein House: Location: Mamaroneck, New York; Assistant: Ken Schiano.

Special Note: Architectural projection system used is fully explained in "Three Projects—John Hejduk," publication—Cooper Union Publications—1968.

### Richard Meier
Smith House: Client: Mr. & Mrs. Fred Smith; Location: Darien, Connecticut; Date of Construction: 1965; Contractor: Ernest Rau; Architect: Richard Meier; Drawings: John Colamarino; Photographs: Ezra Stoller; Publication: The New York Times, April 24, 1966; Architectural Forum, December 1967; The New York Times, February 18, 1968; Domus, April 1968; Architectural Record, Mid-May 1968; The New York Times, June 2, 1968; Interiors, June 1968; Architectural Review, August 1968; House Beautiful, September 1968; Architectural Review, September 1968; House & Home, November 1968; Bauwelt, November 1968; Bauen + Wohnen, November 1968; Holiday, April 1969; Toshi-Jutaka, April 1969; House Beautiful, Summer 1969; A.I.A. Journal, June 1969; Art Today, (Holt, Reinhart & Winston) Faulkner, Ziegfield—1969; Connecticut Architect, September-October 1969; Abitare, October 1969; Connaissance des Arts, March 1970; Decorative Art in Modern Interiors, 1971; Architectural Design, January 1971; Architectural Design, August 1971; "History of Notable American Houses" by Marshall B. Davidson, American Heritage Publishing Co.; "Architecture in a Revolutionary Era" by Julian E. Kulski; Global Interior #1, Houses in the U.S.A. by Yukio Futagawa.
Saltzman House: Client: Mr. & Mrs. Renny B. Saltzman; Location: Easthampton, New York; Date of Construction: 1967; Architect: Richard Meier; Assistants: Carl Meinhardt, Tod Williams; Drawings: John Colamarino, Henry Smith-Miller; Photographs: Ezra Stoller; Publication: House & Garden, December 1969; Progressive Architecture, April 1970; Domus, June 1970; House & Home, November 1970; Bauen + Wohnen, December 1970; Villa Giardini, November 1971, Global Interior #1, Houses in the U.S.A. by Yukio Futagawa.

# Biographies

Peter Eisenman was born in Newark, New Jersey in 1932. He is an architect and Director of The Institute for Architecture and Urban Studies in New York City. He has taught at the University of Cambridge, Princeton, and at present at The Cooper Union. In addition to a series of single family houses which he has designed and built, he has worked on several urban design projects; one for the Manhattan waterfront which was exhibited at the Museum of Modern Art in 1967. He has just completed work on a three year study of the urban street commissioned by the U.S. Department of Housing and Urban Development.

Michael Graves was born in Indianapolis, Indiana, in 1934. He received his training in Architecture at the University of Cincinnati and at Harvard University. He was awarded the Prix de Rome in 1960 and studied at the American Academy in Rome for two years. Graves is Professor of Architecture at Princeton University, where he has taught since 1962. He has also served as Visiting Professor at the University of Texas and has lectured on his work throughout the country. Graves is also in private practice and has completed a variety of projects, including private residences, public housing, museums, medical facilities, and town planning. Among these, his Rockefeller House won a "Progressive Architecture" design award in 1970. His work has been represented in the Museum of Modern Art in two exhibitions; "The New City," 1967, and both his Newark Museum Project and Union County Museum were shown in "The Architecture of Museums," 1968. Graves was one of six architects selected to represent the United States at XV Triennale in Milan, Italy, in 1973. His work has appeared in many periodicals as well as three recent books: *American Art and Architecture of the 20th Century, Architettura Razionale,* and the Japanese publication, *Global Interiors.*

Charles Gwathmey is 37 years old. He was born in 1938 in Charlotte, North Carolina. He attended the University of Pennsylvania School of Architecture from 1956 to 1959 and Yale University School of Architecture from 1959 to 1962 where he received his Bachelor of Architecture Degree. Upon graduation, he received the William Wirt Win-

chester Traveling Fellowship and a Fulbright Grant, and studied for a year in Paris. In 1970, after four years of practice, he received the Arnold Brunner Prize from the National Institute of Arts and Letters. He has taught at Pratt Institute, Yale, Columbia, Princeton, Cooper Union and Harvard. The office which is now Gwathmey Siegel Architects is still doing residences but has also just completed the Student Residential Complex and Dining Facility at the State University at Purchase, New York, the Service Facility and Boiler Plant for the same University, Whig Hall at Princeton University, and is now working on three housing projects for the Urban Devlopment Corporation and a new Physical Education Facility Building at Edgemont School, New York.

John Hejduk was born in New York City in 1929. He was a Fulbright scholar in Italy in 1953. He is an architect and Chairman of the Department of Architecture at The Cooper Union in New York City. He has taught at the University of Texas, Cornell and Yale. He has exhibited his work at the Architectural League of New York, and at the Fondation LeCorbusier, Paris. His "Diamond" projects have been published by The Cooper Union in 1968. He was the recipient of a Graham Foundation Fellowship and The National Endowment of the Arts Award 1972.

Richard Meier was born in Newark, New Jersey in 1934. He received his training in Architecture at Cornell University. He established his own office in New York in 1963. In addition to private residences, Richard Meier has designed a Health and Physical Education Facility for the State University College at Fredonia; the Monroe State School at Rochester and the Bronx State School, both presently under construction for the Health and Mental Hygiene Facilities Improvement Corporation; 500 units of housing at Twin Parks Northeast in the Bronx for The Urban Development Corporation, recently completed; industrial buildings in New Jersey; and the Westbeth Artists Housing in New York. Currently in progress are branch offices and a dormitory building for the Olivetti Corporation of America. Richard Meier has received Honor Awards from The American Institute of Architects. In addition, he was awarded the Arnold Brunner Memorial Prize by the National Institute of Arts and Letters in 1972.

# Postscript

## Philip Johnson

There seems little sense in assembling these *five* architects in *one* book. They no doubt felt they would collectively receive more exposure as five than as five ones. They were right. As five, they have been attacked and defended, praised and vilified.

In common, all they *have* is talent; they are interested, as artists millennia before them have been, in the art of architecture. I feel especially close to them in this world of functionalist calculation and sociometric fact research. I too, a generation ago, was brought up in a period of functionalist movement, that time a revolt against the Beaux Arts. The last line of *The International Style,* which came out in 1933, was what we thought as a triumph: "We have an architecture still." Well, we still do.

Second, I feel close because I too have had my non-revolutionary, eclectic, copying moods, my doubts of where we are at.

If they be too young for me really to understand them, at least I can express a certain empathy and sympathy.

Alphabetically, Peter Eisenman, weighted down by erudition and intellection, nevertheless is most original in his search. Not being able to follow the tortuous path of his prose thoughts, I look at House II, for example, and rejoice in its interpenetrating richness. Rigid complexity is all anyone can hope for. What would he do in a large building?

Michael Graves, a painter–architect heavy with Le Corbusier, in the Hanselmann house miraculously makes 3D paintings come alive. His Benecerraf pavilion is a wonderfully sporty piece of lawn sculpture. If Juan Gris had been a sculptor, he would have rejoiced. Some say the pavilion is a useless structure. Change the word "building" to "sculpture" if that makes the critics feel better.

Charles Gwathmey is a builder (in the sense of Mies' highest compliment: "That building is built!"). His geometric juxtapositions are bludgeon-like clear, his shifts of axis, his warping of the scale sufficiently disturbing to cause the observer pleasant jitters. What will he do for us next year?

John Hejduk is, so far in his career, a theoretician's designer. Not in words — he is a quiet man — but in magnificent drawings. His "wall" house could have (it never will be built) the eerie feeling of Hadrian at Tivoli or Mies' 1923 Brick House: endless walls with squiggles. Geometry again, but isolated, clear, simple. What would they look like at full scale?

Richard Meier, the most traditional of our five youngsters, makes the most "acceptable" houses. The Smith house has already in eight short years become a classic. Meier once had the scale model of Le Corbusier's Savoye House in his living room (I had the Farnsworth House most assuredly in my mind's eye in 1948). What would Le Corbusier say, who at the end of his life so hated his buildings of the 20's, which these architects use as their models?

Meier knows his history best of the five, studies it most, learns from it most. His recent designs for Olivetti U.S.A. give great promise, but life (for an architect) begins at 45. The new (non-Corbusier) direction has begun? is beginning?

One could wish for further books, more work by these architects; perhaps on "Three Architects," "Eight Architects," and so on by other architects as disparate as these. Books call attention to architecture, force the reader (viewer) to focus, and generally arouse amusement or disgust.

Philip Johnson
April 1, 1974